LEEANN BROWETT

TECHNOLOGICALLY IMPAIRED TEENS

AND THE SOFT SKILLS WE NEED TO TEACH THEM TO SUCCEED

outskirts press
DENVER, COLORADO

Teachers have permission to reproduce ready-to-use activities,
rubrics and assessments for student use in the classroom.

Outskirts Press, Inc.
http://www.outskirtspress.com

ISBN: 978-1-4787-5156-4

Outskirts Press and the "OP" logo are trademarks belonging to Outskirts Press, Inc.

PRINTED IN THE UNITED STATES OF AMERICA

For my students,
past, present, and future

CONTENTS

INTRODUCTION

The Internet, Lenin, and Cupcakes

The Internet, smartphones, and personal devices are wonderfully useful technological inventions. They allow us to shop, bank, and even work in our own homes. Information is readily available and, in an instant, we can video chat with family and friends across the globe. The convenience these forms of technology provide seems unlimited. In many ways, they can enhance student learning in our classrooms. So if some use of the Internet, smartphones, and personal devices is good, more use must be better, right? Well, not exactly.

The first time I questioned the benefits of the Internet in education was in the fall of 1999. I was teaching an honors level freshman modern European history class. We were in the midst of a Russian Revolution unit and students were analyzing the impact of Vladimir Lenin's leadership. Having traveled to the former Soviet Union with my own high school chorus in 1989, I described how pictures and statues of Lenin were everywhere. Lenin was worshipped and treated almost God-like. Soviet children came up to me repeatedly wanting to trade button pins for American gum. Twenty-five years later I still have those button pins and almost all of them have a picture of Lenin on them. I described my experience viewing Lenin's body in his tomb in Red Square. After waiting in line for almost two hours in the rain, guards permitted a handful of people at a time to enter the tomb. We could not bring backpacks, cameras, or anything at all in with us. The guards instructed us to walk quickly and silently, with our hands by our sides around the roped off glass sarcophagus containing Lenin's body. I shared that I thought Lenin looked pale and creepy floating in what I assumed was some type of formaldehyde solution. At the same time, I felt awed being in such close proximity to the man that ushered in Soviet communism. The Soviets revered Lenin, how could I not feel humbled?

Students asked what happened to Lenin's body after the Soviet Union collapsed. Was Lenin's body still on display in Red Square? The truth was I didn't know the answer. I told my students I knew at one point there was discussion about burying Lenin's body, but I was not sure what the Russian government decided to do. I offered two points extra credit on the next quiz to the first three students who could accurately determine where Lenin's body was. There were twenty-three enthusiastic freshmen in that honors level modern European history class. When I arrived at my desk the next morning, I was greeted by seventeen paper responses from students as to the whereabouts of Lenin's body. I read the first response and was horrified. I quickly scanned each of the remaining sixteen responses and was in a state of disbelief. Each of those seventeen honors level students printed out information from the same website that indicated Lenin's body was on tour and could be rented for a fee. I cannot remember the exact fee, but as I recall, it was several thousand dollars. The website showed a map with the locations of the various proms, homecoming dances, weddings, and bar/bat mitzvahs where Lenin's body visited. How could my students actually think this information was valid? The words "cupcake" and "canasta" were in the website's URL! That alone should have made my students question the website's reliability, but apparently not. By the way, there is a current blog with the URL "cupcakecanasta.blogspot.com." [1] This blog was created in 2002 and I am not certain if it is connected to the original website my students viewed in 1999. I suspect it may be, given the blog's content.

I was determined to make this a teachable moment. I walked into class prepared to talk to my students about strategies to determine a website's reliability. Although this would be a routine conversation to have with students today, in 1999 this conversation was novel. Before I could begin, my enthusiastic freshmen announced they wanted to rent Lenin's body for their junior prom scheduled in two years and began brainstorming fundraising ideas. Although they were a bit crest-fallen when I told them the website was intended to be humorous and Lenin's body could not be rented, overall my students were able to laugh at themselves and find humor in the situation. I gave my students suggestions on how to determine a website's reliability. Fittingly, on the last day of class I baked cupcakes for my students. On the top of each chocolate frosted cupcake I wrote a letter "T" with lime green icing. As I distributed the cupcakes, I told my students the "T" represented the word "Think". Each and every time they go on the Internet I want them to *think* and use their very capable brains to discern what information is valid and what is not. Over the next few years, I created and revised a website reliability worksheet that students completed when doing research. My students still use this website reliability worksheet today and it remains a useful tool to help students find credible sources. Naively, I thought I combated the negative effect the Internet could have on my students.

In January 2012, for the second time, I questioned how technology was impacting our children. I accompanied my fifth grade son to his Boy Scout troop's Pinewood Derby race. As any parent who has attended Boy Scout Pinewood Derby races can tell you, much of the event time is spent waiting for your son's car race. Having a lot of energy, the boys run, play, yell, and laugh loudly while waiting. Things were different in January of 2012 though. Many boys sat on benches next to each other without speaking. In most instances the boys were sitting shoulder to shoulder while not uttering a sound. Instead, they were engrossed with their new Christmas gifts -various personal devices. The boys played online games and texted each other. I literally watched two boys sitting next to each other text back and forth. When I gently teased them pointing out they could turn, look at each other, and have an actual conversation, the boys shrugged me off saying texting was cool. As I looked around the room and saw more and more boys engaged in similar behavior, I grew concerned. I wondered how their friendships would change if they chose to interact through a device rather than in person. In this case, the boys were choosing to interact through a device when their friends were sitting right next to them. This struck me as odd.

Like those fifth grade Boy Scouts, in the past few years I have watched my students increasingly choose to interact with devices instead of each other. The detrimental effects are becoming more apparent and I feel it is time for educators to collectively intervene. In this book, I hope to connect teen technological overuse with a lack of essential skill development, often referred to as "soft skills". A lack of this skill development not only manifests in the classroom, but later manifests in the workplace and in everyday life. Through increased collaborative group interactions, activities, and assessments, educators can counter the negative effects of technological overuse and teach students the essential soft skills they will need to succeed in school, the workplace, and in life. This book identifies the interpersonal skills educators need to teach students and, through the use of the *Collaborative Group Rubric*, a method to teach and assess those soft skills. Student activities are included to help elementary and secondary students practice and develop soft skills. The book is broken down into the following sections: 1. An overview of how technological overuse impedes our children's skill development; 2. A summary of how impeded skill development manifests in the workplace and negatively impacts the ability to work collaboratively later in life; 3. An identification of the essential soft skills children and adults need; 4. An explanation of the *Collaborative Group Rubric* assessment tool and suggestions for how it can be used to support student soft skill development; 5. Sample soft skill teacher resources and student activities; 6. Middle and high school level sample collaborative group activities and assessments to encourage soft skill development and counter the detrimental effects of technological overuse; and 7. An adapted *Collaborative Group Rubric: Grades K-5* and sample elementary level collaborative group activities to encourage soft skill development in our younger students. All sample collaborative group activities and assessments are aligned to Common Core State Standards and the College, Career, and Civic Life (C3) Framework Standards from the Nation Council for the Social Studies.

While technological advances make life convenient and more manageable, unlimited technological use is not ideal. There is truth to the adage that there can be too much of a good thing. Chocolate is decadent and splendid. I wouldn't want to live without it, but eating chocolate at every meal wouldn't be a healthy life choice. Technology is the same. We need to teach our children to moderate their use of technology. We need to teach our children that technology can be an amazing tool, but not an extension of who they are. [2] We need to teach our children to coexist with technology without being ruled by it. [3]

CHAPTER 1

Technologically Impaired

Technological advances and increased teen smartphone and personal device use have negatively impacted our students' social interactions and concentration levels. There, I said it. I realize making a statement like this makes me sound like a dinosaur, but I have to be direct. If we do not identify a problem, then we cannot explore solutions. I am advocating for a change in student technological use in schools as part of the solution and an increased willingness on the part of adults to limit children's use of technological devices. Based on my observations and interactions with students in the past few years, additionally, I believe schools need to teach social and collaborative skills to compensate for the lack of face-to face interactions that have resulted from incessant teenage smartphone and personal device use.

I first noticed a distinct change in my students a few years ago. In 2011, I took a year maternity leave to care for my newborn son. Being away from teaching for a full year enabled me to look at my students with a fresh, renewed perspective. When I returned from maternity leave in 2012 I saw a marked difference in student interactions at the high school where I teach. During regular passing times between class periods, for the most part, students acted the same. However, when individual students moved through the school when classes were in session, they behaved very differently. Although school hallways are not densely populated when classes are in session, individual students move through the halls at regular intervals to go to the bathroom, the nurse, the main office, their lockers, etc. In the past when students passed each other during these times, they were likely among the few in the hall. Given it was unlikely the students could pretend they did not see each other, on most occasions the students would acknowledge each other through a look or nod, and often would utter a simple greeting like "Hey."

I noticed these simple student hallway exchanges nearly came to a halt in 2012. Since then, at times when classes are in session typical students moving through the halls look more like this:

- Jerry leaves his classroom, takes a smartphone out of his pocket, walks down the hall listening to music, and is glued to the smartphone screen navigating through texts, Facebook, Twitter, Instagram, Snapchat, etc.
- Jerry passes John in the hall and he is doing the same. Jerry and John don't make eye contact or exchange greetings. Both continue on their individual paths as if completely unaware of one another's existence.
- A few more students pass each other in the hall and do the same. All students appear oblivious of each other and their surroundings.
- Students navigate through their individual, self-created, virtual worlds. Social exchanges are infrequent and technological devices are the tools of social avoidance.

Our high school used to have a policy preventing personal device use and students were not permitted to listen to MP3 players during the school day. Around the time smartphones were introduced and personal devices could access the school's wireless network, our school changed its policy and permitted student personal device use in the classroom at the teacher's discretion. The "at the teacher's discretion" part didn't seem to be absorbed by students though. Many students felt entitled to use their personal technology whenever they pleased. When it became necessary to instruct students to take their ear buds out and turn off their music during class activities, some even protested saying the administration permitted their use. I promptly clarified this misconception and students begrudgingly complied with my instructions. However, I was disheartened by the fact students believed technology was their natural born right. I'm fairly certain incessant personal device use is not what John Locke meant by 'right to property'.

When I allowed students to listen to music with ear buds while working independently on individual class assignments, I found students spent more time searching for specific songs online or misused their devices by checking their texts, email, and social media accounts. It was clear students were distracted by their devices. More of my time was spent managing student personal technological use than supporting student learning and I was increasingly frustrated. I was not alone. To illustrate how prevalent this problem became, our school chose to adopt a report card comment code "Distracted by Personal Technology." Technology wasn't supporting student learning, it was impeding student learning. I decided to make a change.

I banned the use of personal technological devices in my classroom. Unless explicitly told they could use their personal devices for a specific academic task, students knew their devices had to remain in their backpacks for the class period. I explained that I witnessed student concentration and focus levels decline when they used personal technology and, as a result, their personal devices were off-limits during class time. I expected my students to protest. Surprisingly, although most were not thrilled with my decision, there wasn't a big backlash. When I explained the personal device ban to parents at a beginning of the year Back to School Night, I also expected parents to protest given they are often texting and instant messaging their children during the school day. Much to my surprise, parents were not only supportive, but most were even thrilled. One group of parents actually applauded when I announced the personal device ban. Once again, foolishly enough, I thought I had conquered technology's negative impact on my students. The reality is I barely scratched the surface.

I should be clear. I am not anti-technology. In many ways technology supports and enhances student learning. I oppose the unlimited use of smartphones and personal devices in school because they impede student focus and learning as well as their social interactions. Most teenage students utilize social media, and in doing so, they appear to be socializing. However, social media is not a substitute for face-to-face social interactions. In the past, teens were notorious for talking on the phone. Social media isn't even an adequate substitute for that. At least tone and volume can be heard and interpreted in a phone conversation. Those are missing in social media. Instant messaging, texting, and group chats have replaced face-to-face and conversational teen social interactions. In 2010 the Pew Research Center cited 54% of teens text their friends at least once a day, but only 3% talked to their friends in person daily. [1] Undoubtedly, those numbers have increased since the study was conducted.

Social media use has changed the way our children communicate. Instead of talking to their friends, today's teens exchange abbreviated text language snatches on cell phones, smartphones, and personal devices. [2] They interface unceasingly on social networks like Facebook and Twitter, and expect constant, frequent responses to their texts, posts, and tweets.[3] Many teens experience FOMO (Fear Of Missing Out) if they are unconnected [4] and when they use smartphones and personal devices, their access to the Internet moves with them throughout the day. [5] With such unhindered Internet access, teens ceaselessly check their texts, email, and social media accounts throughout the school day. If they have a message, they feel compelled to respond NOW as if an apocalypse will descend upon us all if they do not. This impacts teens outside of school as well. Have you had the pleasure of waiting while a teen cashier completes a text or checks Twitter prior to ringing up your shopping order? I have experienced this on several occasions. The teacher in me wanted to address the unprofessional behavior, but I stifled a verbal response and reminded myself that this teenage worker was not my student. On one occasion, instead of verbally correcting the teen's behavior, I alternated between looking directly at the teen and looking at her smartphone. I hoped my eye contact and body language would send the teen the message that texting instead of ringing up customers was inappropriate. Given the teen never made eye contact with me, I'm certain my nonverbal message was not received.

I haven't even addressed the impact instantaneous and incessant teen technological communications have had on student writing. Many students write the way they text, instant message, and tweet. I have to remind students that "LOL," "LMAO," and other forms of slang language do not constitute formal writing. Granted, "sucks," "pissed-off," and "crap" aren't egregious curse words or phrases, but they are inappropriate in formal writing. My students use these words and phrases increasingly. I feel ancient when I remind my students that the language they choose is a reflection of them. To encourage my students to write more formally, I have asked them "Why degrade yourselves and choose to write "pissed-off" instead of language that more accurately reflects your intelligence?" With spell check and autocorrect, many students believe accurate spelling is unnecessary and outdated. Why learn to spell a word correctly if a personal device can fix a spelling error?

Instantaneous technological communications are impeding students' ability to write analytically as well. When texting and instant messaging, student respond quickly without much reflection or supporting detail. When tweeting, students must condense their thoughts to a 140 character message. Both are negatively impacting student writing. When given writing prompts in school, many students write similar curt responses that lack depth, support, and connections between ideas. For example, if a writing prompt asked students to select the most important president in United States history and justify their choice, a student might choose Franklin Delano Roosevelt. In his written response, the student might identify FDR as the most important president and write "because he was a boss" as one of his reasons. The student might also write how Roosevelt handled the Great Depression and World War II as additional reasons, but give little specific factual support from either historical time and fail to draw connections between the Great Depression and World War II. Once, when I questioned a student about his use of slang language and lack of depth and connectivity in his writing, the student responded "You know what I meant." Humorously, I suggested I might consider mind reading as a second profession, but for time being, the student needed to *write* what he meant.

Increased technological use has made physical writing challenging for some students as well. Teens regularly type and touch responses on a screen, but actually *write* with a pen on paper less often. After an essay test, students have left my class complaining their "hand was going to fall off." Few Millenials are taught to write in cursive in school either. Those who have proctored the SATs, know this first-hand. When completing the information portion of the SAT answer sheet, students are required to write a statement in cursive certifying they are the person whose name, address, and signature appear on the answer sheet. It is both torturous and somewhat humorous to watch students struggle to physically write in cursive.

For those who believe social media, texting, and even email promote social interactions, I would argue the quality of those social interactions is greatly diminished. Face-to-face interactions require intimacy and emotional give and take. With reduced exposure to facial expressions and body language, teens' ability to understand emotional nuances and read social cues is impacted. [6] Additionally, teens are developing a false impression that there is a constant Internet audience watching their every move in life. [7] No, it is not necessary to post that you bought a mocha latte at Dunkin Donuts. That is not news-worthy information to share. No one cares. Today's teens live their lives on a virtual stage. As a result, their empathy decreases and narcissism increases. [8]

Smartphone and personal device use can be an avoidance strategy. [9] It certainly seems like one when I watch the students move through the halls during class time. Many teens text and email to avoid confrontations and uncomfortable social situations. [10] [11] Although that may seem easier, in doing so teens are not getting the opportunity to practice how to deal with uncomfortable situations in person. How will that impact their future interactions with colleagues, bosses, and significant others? My students regularly email me requesting time extensions for projects, information about what they missed when they were absent, and asking if I will read a rough draft essay far more often than they ask me those questions in person.

The Kaiser Family Foundation of America recently found that children between the ages of 8 and 18 spend an average of 7 ½ hours a day using some sort of electronic device. [12] That is more time than most children spend in school or even sleeping. With that much time being spent glued to electronic screens, children's creativity, imagination, and self-initiation suffer. [13] When I assign tasks that require students to use their imaginations, like creating a political cartoon that reflects the significance of a historical event, my students frequently ask me for help. This is a particular issue at the beginning of the school year and the "help" students seem to want involves me using *my* imagination to spoon-feed ideas to them. Creating a political cartoon is a higher order thinking activity that requires students to demonstrate historical understanding and interpretation, visual symbolism, and an editorial point of view with humor and/or sarcasm. It is a challenging activity and it is meant to be. I teach the components of political cartoons and we interpret several political cartoons as a class prior to students being asked to create political cartoons on their own. Since using my creativity to enable students defeats the purpose of a political cartoon assignment, I explain to students that they need to use *their* brains and not mine. Then I assist students by asking questions, often starting with questions that tap into key aspects of the historical event and students' opinion of those aspects. I graduate to questions that encourage students to think about how to represent that information visually and humorously. Many of today's teens need help tapping into their own creativity.

Developmentally, middle school, high school, and college age young adults struggle with forming their own identities. Today they have to struggle with digital identity issues when their actual identities have not been fully formed. [14] Pictures and images can also spread like wildfire on the Internet. A teacher wanted to demonstrate this exact point to her junior high school students. She took a picture of herself holding a sign that said "I want to illustrate to my junior high students (grades 7-9) how fast a photo can be shared on the Internet. Please "Like" and "Share" this image to help me teach caution and discernment to the students in my classes." [15] On November 29, 2013 Fox 9 News based in Eden Prairie, Minnesota shared the teacher's photo on Facebook. Eight months later, the teacher's photo was reshared on Facebook 2,730,055 times. Remember your middle school years? They were brutal, right? Honestly, you couldn't pay me to re-live mine. Now imagine those years permanently and publically documented with photos on the Internet. That is one scary thought. At least I alone have access to the photos of my frizzy-haired layered bob, neon yellow sweater vest with matching belt and socks, and two-toned jeans look of 1984. I am forever thankful those photos won't be permanently floating in cyberspace.

Questions have been raised as to whether such avid electronic use is re-wiring children's brains.[16] So how prevalent is teenage cell phone, smartphone, and personal device use? Teen cell phone use rose dramatically from 2004, when 45% of teens used their cell phones daily, to 2010, when 75% of teens used their cell phones daily. [17] That 30% increase in six years is significant, and suggests some cultural or technological change. Looking back, the introduction of touchscreen smartphones in 2007 may be the change that caused such a dramatic increase in teenage cell phone use. I distinctly remember one of my twelfth grade students telling me she waited in line for hours to be one of the first people to purchase one in June 2007. She enthusiastically showed me how it worked. Truth be told, her enthusiasm was infectious.

Teen cell phone and smartphone use has continued to rise since 2010. According to a Pew Research study conducted in 2012, 78% of young adults between the ages of twelve and seventeen have cell phones, 47% of which are smartphones. The total percentage of American teens with smartphones was 37% in 2012. This is a significant increase from the 23% of American teens having smartphones in 2011. [18] Seventy-four percent of teens access the Internet through smartphones, tablets, or other mobile devices like iPods. While this percentage may appear high, I found it interesting that the percentage of adults under the age of 50 that access the Internet through smartphones, tablets, and other mobile devices is identical. [19] One in four teens are "cell-mostly" Internet users and one in four teens have a tablet computer to access the Internet. [20] Undoubtedly, the percentage of teens that have and use smartphones today is significantly higher. A 2013 Neilson.com survey estimated 70% of teens own smartphones. [21] Unquestionably, teen cell phone and smartphone use is on the rise and will likely continue to escalate.

Along with the compelling rise in teen cell phone, smartphone, and personal devise use, is the rise in teenage texting. Thirty-eight percent of teens texted daily in 2008. That percentage rose to

54% in 2010. [22] In 2012 the average American, regardless of age, sent and received 400 texts per month, four times as many texts as in 2007. [23] In comparison, in 2012 the average teen sent and received 3,700 texts per month. [24] That means the average American teen sends and receives 122 texts per day, clearly confirming American teens expect and participate in frequent, instant contact. The nature of teen communication and, likely, their friendships have changed. We have a no cell phone or personal device at the table during meals rule in our home. Although my teenage son's cell phone isn't physically with him at the table, he can hear it ping when he receives a text during dinner. While he complies with our rule and doesn't respond to the text, he clearly looks agitated that he cannot respond. The moment he is finished eating and puts his dishes in the dishwasher, he dashes to his phone to see who texted him so he can respond.

Teen smartphone use seems pandemic and will likely continue to expand exponentially. Its use transcends socioeconomic distinctions. When compared, teenage demographic groups use smartphones in similar capacities. According to the Pew research study conducted in 2012, 27% of urban teens are "cell-mostly" Internet users. Similarly, 24% of suburban teens and 21% of rural teens are "cell-mostly" Internet users. [25] However, it is important to note that African American teens are more likely to be "cell-mostly" Internet users. Thirty-three percent of African American teens, as compared to 24% of Caucasian teens and 21% of Hispanic teens are "cell-mostly" Internet users. [26] Similarly, teenage girls show a stronger preference to communicate with technology. [27] [28] While the negative impact of smartphone use on social skills and focus transcends teenage demographics, African American teens and young women are likely among the most impacted. Although there are no definitive answers as to why this is the case, concerns have been raised that African Americans and women are not advancing professionally to the highest echelon in the workplace and that they are unable to earn equal pay for equal work. It would seem detrimental for both groups to stymie their focus and social skills, which could later impact their already challenging professional advancements.

So, American teens use smartphones and personal devices constantly. As a result, their social interactions, focus, and ability to concentrate suffer. Why? Smartphones and personal devices are like electronic cocaine, every ping or vibration physically increases dopamine levels in the brain. [29] Chronic electronics users often experience manic periods followed by depression. They are anxious and can act impulsively. Chronic Internet use fosters obsession, dependency, and stress reactions. [30] The prefrontal cortex of the brain in avid Internet users looks like that of the brain in drug and alcohol abusers. [31] The brain's structural gray matter, responsible for processing speed, memory, motor control, emotions, and sensory information, decreases 10-20% when chronic Internet use occurs, and the shrinkage doesn't appear to be reversible. Chronic Internet use has been linked to increased Obsessive Compulsive Disorder and Attention Deficit Hyperactivity Disorder. [32] Two-thirds of cell phone users even experience "phantom vibration syndrome." They feel their phones vibrate when no vibration actually occurs. [33] Except for those over the age of 50, most Internet users text and check their email or social media accounts "all the time," which is defined as a minimum of every fifteen minutes. [34] That is incredibly time consuming. Further confirming the concept that Internet use is addicting is the fact that the most recent Diagnostic and Statistical Manual of Mental Disorders

(DSM 5) has added "Internet Addiction Disorder" to its mental disorders list. [35] Any day now, we'll see a twelve step program for Internet abuse.

Adding to the concern that pronounced Internet use is damaging, a 2011 study found people's self-esteem levels decrease as the frequency of Facebook use and status update posts increase. [36] In social media, people likely present their lives in a far more positive light than they actually may be. People create social media narratives for a public audience, but I question how honest those narratives are. I have seen many pictures posted of happy families in happy moments. I am guilty of doing this too. However, I don't post pictures of my toddler melting down because he can't get the hood of his toy car to stay open. Therefore, my posts don't always accurately represent my daily life. When our teens chronically access social media through smartphones and personal devices, they are exposing themselves to less-than-honest, self-created narratives that, in many cases, cause them to feel like they don't measure up. Their lives aren't nearly as exciting, their boyfriends or girlfriends aren't nearly as romantic, and their parents aren't buying them nearly as many gadgets. When they constantly access social media posts, teens are setting themselves up for unrealistic expectations and further putting themselves at emotional risk.

If teens spend copious amounts of time interfacing with smartphones and personal devices and obsessively respond to their every ping, they have less time to interact with real people. Common sense dictates if teens invest less time interacting with people, their social skills will diminish. No matter what a teenager may tell you, interacting with a personal device is not the same as interacting with a person. Personal interactions provide you with far more information to interpret and react to than a text or social media post. Face-to-face interactions can be subtle, compelling, and powerful. [37] They require people to take into account facial expressions, body language, and tone of voice. A simple look or gesture can say as much as a well-crafted sentence. Additionally, you need to think on your feet and respond appropriately when you interact with a real person in real time. If you misinterpret, hurt, or offend a person you cannot avoid his response. You have to deal with it because that person is literally staring you in the face.

A 2013 Connecticut College undergraduate study of 18 to 23 year olds indicated those who prefer to communicate technologically show diminished facial expressions and nod less frequently when interacting in person. Additionally, they encourage their speaking partners less. [38] If you constantly invest your time on the Internet, you are more likely to miss non-verbal cues like fidgeting, foot tapping, long pauses, and varying degrees of eye contact. [39] Those cues are necessary to interpret communication and respond according. Social and emotional skill development is the casualty of technological overuse. Technologically dependent children have trouble initiating interactions with others and become more detached from their friends and family. [40] My students reported having difficulty interacting with collaborative group members who were not in their close circle of friends. Teachers and parents in partnership need to be proactive and deliberate in encouraging the benefits of technology, while managing technology's potentially harmful effects. One parent and author did exactly that. Along with an iPhone, *Huffington Post* writer Janell Burley Hofmann gave her thirteen-year-old son a contract. The iPhone contract consisted of the following rules:

1. "It is my phone. I bought it. I pay for it. I am loaning it to you. Aren't I the greatest?

2. I will always know the password.

3. If it rings, answer it. It is a phone. Say hello, use your manners. Do not ever ignore a phone call if the screen reads "Mom" or "Dad." Not ever.

4. Hand the phone to one of your parents promptly at 7:30 p.m. every school night and every weekend night at 9:00 p.m. It will be shut off for the night and turned on again at 7:30 a.m. If you would not make a call to someone's land line, wherein their parents may answer first, then do not call or text. Listen to those instincts and respect other families like we would like to be respected.

5. It does not go to school with you. Have a conversation with the people you text in person. It's a life skill. *Half days, field trips and after school activities will require special consideration.

6. If it falls into the toilet, smashes on the ground, or vanishes into thin air, you are responsible for the replacement costs or repairs. Mow a lawn, babysit, stash some birthday money. It will happen, you should be prepared.

7. Do not use this technology to lie, fool, or deceive another human being. Do not involve yourself in conversations that are hurtful to others. Be a good friend first or stay the hell out of the crossfire.

8. Do not text, email, or say anything through this device you would not say in person.

9. Do not text, email, or say anything to someone that you would not say out loud with their parents in the room. Censor yourself.

10. No porn. Search the web for information you would openly share with me. If you have a question about anything, ask a person -- preferably me or your father.

11. Turn it off, silence it, put it away in public. Especially in a restaurant, at the movies, or while speaking with another human being. You are not a rude person; do not allow the iPhone to change that.

12. Do not send or receive pictures of your private parts or anyone else's private parts. Don't laugh. Someday you will be tempted to do this despite your high intelligence. It is risky and could ruin your teenage/college/adult life. It is always a bad idea. Cyberspace is vast and more powerful than you. And it is hard to make anything of this magnitude disappear -- including a bad reputation.

13. Don't take a zillion pictures and videos. There is no need to document everything. Live your experiences. They will be stored in your memory for eternity.

14. Leave your phone home sometimes and feel safe and secure in that decision. It is not alive or an extension of you. Learn to live without it. Be bigger and more powerful than FOMO (fear of missing out).

15. Download music that is new or classic or different than the millions of your peers that listen to the same exact stuff. Your generation has access to music like never before in history. Take advantage of that gift. Expand your horizons.

16. Play a game with words or puzzles or brain teasers every now and then.

17. Keep your eyes up. See the world happening around you. Stare out a window. Listen to the birds. Take a walk. Talk to a stranger. Wonder without googling.
18. You will mess up. I will take away your phone. We will sit down and talk about it. We will start over again. You and I, we are always learning. I am on your team. We are in this together."[41]

I applaud Ms. Hofmann's efforts. She sees the potentially negative impact of her son's smartphone use and is willing to do what many parents and teachers are not: limit a child's technological use. Ms. Hoffman isn't trying to win a popularity contest with her son. She is stepping up and being a parent. Her rules are reasonable and necessary. By implementing them, she is guiding and supporting her son. We, as a society, have to conquer the fallacy that technology means advancement all the time. Are there many benefits of smartphones and personal devices? Absolutely. Are there many benefits of the Internet? Of course. Who wants to return to the days of card catalogs and microfiche, when research involved driving to libraries in multiple towns hoping to find a useful source? I know I don't. Yet we must accept that just because something has benefits, doesn't mean it should be utilized obsessively. Like most things in life, the Internet and personal technology need to be used in moderation. Our children are becoming enslaved by their smartphones and personal devices. We are the adults. It is our job to intervene. If our guidelines are unpopular, so be it. If we don't intervene, the impact of smartphone and personal device use will not only negatively impact our children's friendships, social skills, and focus in school, but it will impede their ability to function successfully in the workforce.

CHAPTER 2

Hard and Soft

Internet, smartphone, and personal device overuse detrimentally impact our children's chances of functioning successfully in the workforce. As children spend more time interacting with personal devices and less time interacting with people, their social skills suffer. In fact, technological overuse impedes the development of our children's soft skills. Soft skills are needed to navigate the workplace successfully. [1] They are the attitudes and behaviors that correlate with career success, enabling people to work effectively without friction. [2] Having strong interpersonal skills, a positive attitude, good teamwork skills, and the ability to competently prioritize work all fall under the umbrella of soft skills. [3] In short, soft skills are a representation of one's emotional intelligence. [4]

Soft skills are differentiated from hard skills, which are the skill set required to perform a specific job or task. [5] Hard skills in education could include planning, instructing, and assessing students. Possessing a sophisticated understanding of the content in the disciple specific courses taught is a hard skill. Infusing Common Core standards in curriculum is a hard skill. In contrast, soft skills are more closely linked to the *art* of teaching. An accomplished teacher with strong soft skills doesn't encourage, but rather, *inspires* her students to learn. She is passionate about what she teaches and that passion is infectious. Her students know and feel she cares about them and believes they can achieve. She can read her students' emotions well, and knows when to push her students further and when to offer them more support. She uses humor and is tuned into the developmental idiosyncrasies of her students. With a look or a phrase she can reassure students and parents alike. Students want to talk to their soft skills teachers before and after class about school and life outside of school. These teachers collaborate well with fellow teachers and are often consensus builders. Colleagues enjoy working with them and often go to them for advice.

A truly talented teacher has strong hard *and* soft skills. A teacher that has strong hard skills, but lacks soft skills, will likely never be more than mediocre. Similarly, a teacher with strong soft skills and poor hard skills performs superficially at a sub-par level. In short, a combination of hard and soft skills is necessary for teaching success. The same can be said about career success. Successful employees must have a combination of both hard and soft skills.

Historically, as educators, we have supported our students' development of hard skills. We teach students how to read, write, mathematically problem solve, and the content of our discipline specific courses. Our students analyze documents and determine an author's purpose. Organizing an essay centered on a focused claim that is supported by body paragraphs with facts and analysis is what we teach our students to do. Students determine which mathematical equation is best to solve a numeric-based problem. Common Core Standards are infused mainly with hard skills. Undoubtedly, teaching students educational hard skills is essential. Many would likely say that, in fact, teaching hard skills is the purpose of education. Given the negative impact of teenage technological overuse on social skills and concentration, teaching students soft skills may very well become equally essential. Recent polls and surveys suggest that employers and managers would agree.

Employers and managers are becoming more and more unimpressed with Millennial, or Generation Y, job applicants. Many of the social skills and concentration capabilities that are deteriorating as a result of teen technological overuse comprise the soft skills employers want to see in their workers. When interviewing a potential employee, employers and managers look for a strong work ethic, positive attitude, good communication and time management skills, confidence, the ability to prioritize important items, knowledge of when to delegate tasks, and the ability to get things done within the confines of available resources. [6] A recent Center for Professional Excellence annual survey of over 400 human resource executives found that young employees exude arrogance and a sense of entitlement at work.[7] While they may have bold online profiles, young job applicants often fail to make eye contact, do not carry themselves well, and do not speak with confidence. [8] A small number of Millennials use casual and slang language during interviews. Some Millennials even respond to a text message or take a phone call during an interview. [9] I find this shocking. You would think Millennials would refrain from texting and taking a phone call at a time when they should be on their best behavior and ultra-conscious of the impression they are making. I guess not. It is as if they are unaware of the people around them, much like the students passing each other in our high school hallways during class time. Yet if we don't prevent, or at minimum, deter teens from behaving this way in our schools, why would they behave differently in the workplace later in life? Some Millennials have their parents accompany them on interviews. [10] I cannot think of a better way to convey incapability, inadequacy, and dependency to a potential employer than to bring Mommy or Daddy in tow to an interview. I am stunned that an applicant would do this, but I am bewildered why any parent would comply with such a request from a son or daughter. I have two sons and I cannot fathom enabling them in such a fashion. Participating in such codependent behavior can only thwart their independence and retard their sense of self-efficacy. If we want to foster successful adult professional behaviors later in life, parents and educators alike need to teach our children technological boundaries and the soft skills that smartphones and personal devices inhibit.

Employers and managers continue to have reservations about their young employees once hired. A 2013 American Express and Generation Y Research Firm for Millennial Branding survey found that 47% of managers believe Millennial workers have a poor work ethic. Forty-six percent found Millennial workers are easily distracted, relying on constant interactions with technology. [11] After observing high school students do the same in the past few years, I am not surprised. The same study indicated managers believe Millennials lack necessary soft skills, including: good communication, interpersonal interactions, time management skills, and a willingness to work as a team. [12] Common sense suggests Millennials are going to lack these skills; they have been interacting with personal devices instead of people. The American public echoes some of the same concerns as employers and managers. In 2014 the Robert Morris University Polling Institute found 70.3% of Americans worry technological advances are impairing the social skills of young workers. [13] Workers lacking soft skills is not an employment problem confined to the United States. The 2013 Annual Talent Shortage Survey from Manpower Group showed nearly one in five employers worldwide cannot find employees with necessary soft skills. These employers find job candidates lack motivation, interpersonal skills, appropriate appearance, punctuality, and flexibility. [14] A general sense of professionalism seems to evade many potential young workers, and many college graduates have become unemployable because they cannot show up to work on time or dress professionally. [15]

A top complaint of many employers is that young workers lack basic communication skills. When young workers communicate they do so in the same manner they send a text or post on social media sites. Their communications are abbreviated and perfunctory. [16] Young workers need to be able to hold a conversation as well as send and receive emails with professionalism. [17] One Intel campus relations manager believes the writing skills of Millennials have declined because they text more and write less. Writing in complete sentences and articulating professionally no longer seem to be skills of young workers. [18] According to the Workforce Solutions Group at St. Louis Communications College, 60% of employers say job applicants lack communication and interpersonal skills. [19] An Adecco survey found 44% of employers felt soft skill communication was one of the greatest areas of employee weakness. [20] Sixty-two percent of the 770 managers and executives of the American Management Association believe current employees have average to below average communication skills. Clearly, good oral and written communication are weaknesses of young workers. Teenage technological overuse that encourages weak communication is not going to help our children succeed in the workplace. We must find ways to teach social and communication skills in the classroom to help ensure our students' future success.

Collaborative skills, critical thinking, and creativity also top the list of skills lacking in current workers. The same Addeco survey in which 44% of employers identified communication as one of the greatest areas of employee weakness also found collaboration, critical thinking, and creativity to be areas of equal weakness. [21] Sixty-one percent of the 770 managers and executives of the American Management Association believe current workers have average to below average creativity levels; 52% found current workers have average to below average collaboration skills; and 49% found current workers have average to below average critical thinking skills. [22] Given I see some of the same weaknesses in my current students, I am not surprised.

It is when I ask my students to work collaboratively that their lack of soft skills is most apparent. In particular, I observe my students struggling with communication, teamwork, and concentration. In general, my students tell me they like cooperative group work when they can choose their groups and work with their friends, but they feel uncomfortable and awkward if they have to work in groups chosen by me. That makes sense given what I have observed in student hallway interactions. During regular passing times between classes, students act as they always have. They travel from one class to the next with their friends and they are interacting, laughing, and talkative. They are not glued to their personal technological devices. In contrast when students travel the halls during times when classes are in session, they are not traveling with their friends. Students are disconnected and they are consumed with their personal devices. They rarely look up and acknowledge the other students they pass. Perhaps they feel awkward and uncomfortable, just as they do when they have to work in cooperative groups without their friends. Their personal devices provide a mode to escape their discomfort.

While a few of my students tell me they like working in cooperative groups because they are exposed to new ideas and perspectives, overwhelmingly my students do not like working in cooperative groups they have not chosen for themselves. In addition to feeling uncomfortable in these groups, my students indicate they struggle breaking down and dividing project tasks equitably and dealing with "slackers," those group members who do not seem willing to do their fair share of the work. When I asked my students what strategies they use to address a group "slacker," they told me they yell at the "slacker," tell the "slacker" he is doing a terrible job, and dictate to the "slacker" what his tasks are and a deadline for task completion.

Some students completed the work of the "slacker" to avoid getting a bad grade. When I asked my students if these "slacker" strategies were effective, overwhelmingly students told me they were not. "Why would you continue to do something that doesn't work?" I asked. Students were silent. I asked students to think back to an instance when they were yelled at and terms of behavior were dictated to them. I asked them to think about how that made them feel. Did they feel motivated to do what they were told? A chorus of "No" and "Hell no!" responses flowed from my students.

"So why would you think behaving that way would engage a "slacker?"" I asked. Most of my students remained quiet, but their body language and eye contact assured me I had their attention and they were interested. Some were smiling and seemed to understand where I was heading. "What could you do instead?" I asked. As a class we brainstormed ideas. Some class generated "slacker" strategies included: using humor, asking the underperforming classmates if they needed help or if something was preventing them from completing their work, using encouraging language, and acknowledging what the underperforming students had contributed and what they did well. Within a short period of time, less than fifteen minutes, students seemed to understand that the way they approach a person they are having a problem with directly impacts whether or not the problem get resolved.

I was encouraged and felt the time we were spending in class talking about effective communication techniques was helping my students, so I decided to take it a step further. I suggested that sometimes someone that appears to be a "slacker," may simply have a different style of completing work. Some students feel anxious when an assignment is first given and feel motivated to complete a project as soon as possible. Others feel more motivated as an impending deadline nears. "Maybe a "slacker" isn't really a "slacker." Maybe the individual simply has a different style of working." I shared that when I have work to complete I want to get started immediately. If I don't, I feel stressed and I can't relax. My husband, on the other hand, doesn't like to complete work immediately, but feels a surge of energy as a deadline looms. He feels no stress putting the work off and can thoroughly relax and enjoy himself. I shared that in many ways I envied my husband's style. He certainly has lower stress levels than me.

"We are just wired differently and have to figure out how to work together despite that fact. To be honest, sometimes it is difficult, but usually finding the middle ground works for us," I explained. My students started volunteering "I need to get started right away." "I do everything at the last minute," others chimed in. I suggested that might be a useful conversation to have with group members when a collaborative project is first assigned. "If you have different styles, you will need to figure out how to make that work," I told my students. "Either way, you can't make someone work the way you do. Compromise, not control, is the key." Several students made comments about how they hate being in groups with overly controlling people. Some students were honest and admitted they were the control freaks in groups. They shared that they felt uncomfortable trusting others to get work done.

This was a tremendously valuable class discussion. We talked about emotions, how to work together on a team, and respecting each other's individual styles. At times, I felt more like I was leading a group therapy session than a class discussion and the content of what we discussed was nowhere in the curriculum. Given the increasing communication and collaborative weaknesses I was seeing in my students and the fact I was about to assign a collaborative group project, I felt taking the time to encourage this student discussion was the right thing to do.

My intention was to support students and to make the impending collaborative group project a more positive experience for them. Students were open and honest. They were interested and engaged. They seemed to appreciate the advice I gave and the cooperative group strategies we brainstormed together. Their projects, which involved class presentations proposing solutions to current domestic policy issues, were excellent and reflected far greater collaboration than I had witnessed previously in the school year. I chided myself for not initiating a class discussion like this sooner. It was then that I realized if I truly want to support my students and help them develop essential academic and life skills, I need to teach soft skills. It isn't in the curriculum and there is no certification to teach them, but this is what my students need and I won't short change them.

I adore my students. They make going to work each day fun, entertaining, rewarding, and fulfilling. They have a spirit and an energy that is contagious. They make me laugh and they keep me young. They are kind and generous. They must be if they smile and laugh at my corny jokes. My students are salt-of-the-earth good people. I feel the need to say this because I have been critical of today's students. It is not so much that I am critical of our students themselves, but rather critical of the impact constant smartphone and personal device use has had on them and our failure as educators and parents to limit that impact.

We have an obligation to do right by our students. Today so much emphasis is being placed on the hard skill Common Core State Standards to help prepare our students for the future, but we seem to be forgetting the soft skills our students need. Today's employees need a combination of hard and soft skills to succeed, so do our students.

If technological overuse is draining and stunting our students' soft skills, we, as educators and parents, must help our children develop the soft skills needed for future career and personal success. I believe giving our students more opportunities to work in collaborative groups is the best way to help our students develop these necessary soft skills. Collaborative group work requires students to develop and utilize communication and teamwork skills, while at the same time, encouraging critical thinking and creativity. Let me be clear, I am not suggesting that individual student work and accountability be eliminated. I am simply suggesting that through moderately increased collaborative group activities and assessments we can teach our students the communication and teamwork skills they will need for future success. I am suggesting we focus on developing the whole student, not just the academic student. This is no small task. It will require teaching communication and teamwork skills. We need to give students the opportunity to practice these skills, guiding and supporting them as they practice. As educators, we need to commit to developing the whole student, hard *and* soft.

CHAPTER 3

Communication and Teamwork

Communication and teamwork skills are the two most important soft skills we need to teach our students in order to counter the negative effects of technological overuse and sufficiently prepare them for the future. There are multiple components of each. Many of the current student and employee skill weaknesses fall under the skill set umbrella of either communication or teamwork skills.

Communication

If we are going to teach our students how to communicate more effectively, we need to define what good communication looks like. Good communicators are:

1. active listeners,
2. adept at interpreting nonverbal communication,
3. clear and concise,
4. friendly,
5. confident,
6. empathetic,
7. open-minded and flexible,
8. respectful,
9. capable of giving and receiving productive feedback in an assertive manner, and
10. able to choose the most effective mode of communication (e.g., email, in-person conversation, text, letter). [1] [2]

Many of the items on the top ten list of good communicators are self-explanatory. Others, however, need more clarification. For example, active listening is an incredibly useful communication skill if implemented properly. The purpose of active listening is to commit to understanding another's perspective, not simply listening to respond. When one employs active listening strategies, he:

- repeats the speaker's words in order to ensure he heard them correctly,
- summarizes and rephrases the speaker's words in order to confirm understanding,
- asks questions to check for understanding,
- encourages the speaker to elaborate, and
- takes what the speaker says seriously. [3]

In many ways, active listening mirrors conflict resolution. When one employs conflict resolution, he takes active listening a step further. After actively listening to his partner, he defines a problem. Along with his speaking partner, he focuses on a solution and what actions need to be taken to actualize the solution. [4] Regardless of whether one partakes in active listening or conflict resolution, the focus is placed on understanding another person's perspective either to validate the other person or to implement a solution. These are far more sophisticated and effective strategies than the yell at the "slacker" approach my students previously engaged in.

Defining nonverbal communication may seem silly, but given many of our students spend more time staring at smartphone and personal device screens than people, it is necessary. We are far more capable of sensing how someone feels when we are tuned in to their nonverbal communication. [5] When one wants to convey positive nonverbal communication, she:

- keeps her head up and arms uncrossed,
- leans forward,
- makes good eye contact, particularly when speaking,
- uses an audible and appropriate volume when speaking,
- employs a confident, but not arrogant, tone of voice,
- faces a person who is speaking, and
- shows warmth by nodding and smiling at a speaker. [6] [7]

Therefore, doing the opposite conveys dissatisfaction or negative nonverbal communication. When students work collaboratively, it is useful to read each other's body language. If a student exhibits negative nonverbal communication and other collaborative group members recognize this, they can engage the student, identify a problem, and create a solution. If collaborative group members miss the negative nonverbal cues, a problem could fester and later erupt. Skillful students who recognize a group member's negative nonverbal cues can use empathy to further engage the group member, thwart a problem, and exact an agreeable solution. Beginning a conversation with phrases like "I imagine you are probably feeling...," "Tell me what you think about...," "If I heard you correctly...," and "How can we better....?" all help to establish empathy. [8] [9] Addressing a person by name and pausing to leave spaces for a group member to speak are helpful as well.

Being able to give and receive productive feedback in an assertive manner takes practice and maturity. In many ways, it is another method of conflict resolution. Although it should not be critical, productive feedback involves addressing a flaw, weakness, or concern of a collaborative group member. Before students decide to give productive feedback to a group member, they should decide if the battle is worth waging. If the battle is going to cause tension and is not likely to change or resolve a situation, perhaps addressing the concern isn't worth it. If the battle is worth waging, more praise than criticism should be given when providing productive feedback. Suggestions to help students implement productive and assertive feedback include:

- start and end on a positive note,
- be direct and honest, yet tactful and respectful,
- give productive feedback privately to avoid embarrassing someone,
- give timely feedback and focus on one thing, rather than a laundry list of everything you think a group member has done wrong,
- talk about a behavior and not the person,
- try to focus on a solution, not just the problem,
- don't assume you have all the answers and try to create a mutually acceptable solution,
- own your opinion by using "I" not "you" statements,
- avoid absolutes (e.g., "sometimes" is better than "always"),
- keep your emotions under control,
- be open to the other person's perspective and to new information, and
- be aware of any prejudices or misperceptions you have. [10] [11] [12]

While good communication takes practice, maturity, and competence, it is an important life skill. Combined with effective teamwork, good communication better prepares our students for the career and personal challenges they will face in the future.

Teamwork

Good teamwork and good communication are closely linked. As a result there are several overlapping characteristics of the two. The foundation of teamwork is a group working together to achieve a uniform goal. Without a goal, a team has no purpose. For educational purposes a collaborative group's goal is either the teacher generated activity or assessment or a student generated inquiry-based activity or assessment. Effective team players are:

1. active listeners,
2. effective questioners,
3. persuasive and can defend positions logically,
4. problem-solvers,
5. respectful,
6. helpful,
7. cooperative,
8. sharing participants,
9. capable of breaking down a project into smaller tasks, and
10. accountable. [13] [14]

Much like good communicators, effective team players need active listening skills. In order to work cohesively as a team, it is important to fully understand other members' perspectives. Active listening combined with effective questioning is useful when resolving disputes. For example, asking a teammate "Can you help me understand your thinking?" is far more productive than asking "Why did you do that?" [15] The former promotes engagement and understanding, while the latter could elicit a defensive response. Being able to identify a problem and work toward an agreed upon solution is critical in resolving disputes as well.

Being persuasive and making logical arguments are important because these skills help move teams toward consensus when decisions need to be made. In contrast, being overbearing and dictatorial will likely be divisive and impede a team's ability to function. When framing an argument or defending a position, it is important for students to be respectful and mindful of the value of each individual team member. When teammates are helpful, cooperative, and sharing participants, they acknowledge the contributions of others, expand on group members' ideas, give and seek input from others, assist others, ask for help, check for agreement and understanding, and notify teammates of changes in a timely manner. [16] All of these are essential teamwork skills.

When students are assigned group projects, they often dive into the content of the project requirements, but neglect to set up team ground rules. Establishing ground rules will help students define expectations, manage the group project, and most likely, reduce the chances of team disputes. Students can ask the following questions to help establish ground rules for their teams:

- How will we communicate outside of class?;
- Do we have all group members' contact information?;
- How will we make decisions? Through consensus? Majority rule?;
- What are the tasks required to complete this project?;
- How will we distribute tasks among team members? Should any tasks be assigned to individual group members based on their strengths?;
- What are the roles of each team member?;
- When will we meet outside of class?;
- How will we monitor our team's work? [17]

Taking as few as ten minutes to establish ground rules can greatly reduce conflict, uncertainty, and miscommunication. A teacher should maintain the standard that all group members are expected to be equal participants in the collaborative group project. It is important for students to know that they will be held accountable. "Slackers" are not welcome on teams. In truth, academic freeloading is academic dishonesty. [18] If a student puts her name on a project she did not equally contribute to, she is cheating. School academic dishonesty policies should be applied.

Students tell me a challenging aspect of collaborative group projects is finding the time to meet outside of class. This concern is valid. If time permits, allowing students to work collaboratively during class can help to address this concern. In-class collaborative group work time also allows a teacher to monitor team progress and better support students as they develop their soft skills.

CHAPTER 4

Using Collaborative Groups to Teach Soft Skills

Giving students more opportunities to work collaboratively in groups is an effective way to counterbalance the negative impact technological overuse has on soft skill development. When constructed mindfully, collaborative group activities and assessments can help our students tap into their creativity, think critically, and problem solve. In the end, collaborative group activities will better prepare our students to successfully navigate the workplace. This is true of student generated inquiry-based activities and assessments as well. In order for collaborative group experiences to be meaningful and purposeful, we need to take the time to teach our students good communication and teamwork skills. As educators, we must see the connection between the negative effects of technological overuse, the lack of soft skill development that is apparent in school and the workplace, and the benefits of teaching and allowing students to practice soft skills in the classroom. If we can make these connections, we can more effectively support the development of the whole child.

The *Collaborative Group Rubric*, located at the end of this chapter, makes these connections. This rubric is intended to help teachers identify important soft skills in order to teach them more effectively and is designed for middle and high school students. An adapted elementary level rubric is located in Chapter 7. Both rubrics are tools to assess students' soft skill development through the medium of collaborative group work. Essential soft skills have been organized in five categories: Project Management, Communication, Team Work, Problem Solving, and Professionalism.

Project Management

Project Management takes into account our students' struggles with organization and coordinating work outside of class. It encourages students to break down a project into smaller, more manageable tasks and to assign those tasks thoughtfully to individual group members. When Project Management is completed carefully and intentionally, the foundation for a positive collaborative group experience is built. Components of Project Management include:

- sharing contact information,
- choosing a meeting schedule and communication methods,
- determining how group decisions will be made, group member roles, and how group work will be monitored,
- analyzing and prioritizing project tasks, and
- distributing group tasks fairly based on group member strengths.

It may help to have students take a learning styles inventory prior to engaging in collaborative group activities. There are various learning styles inventories available that determine if a person is an auditory, visual, or kinesthetic/tactile learner. Likewise, learning styles inventories can determine if a person's thinking is concrete sequential, concrete random, abstract sequential, or abstract random, a Mind Styles Model established by Dr. Anthony Gregorc. [1] Boise State University provides a free online learning styles inventory and a description of each of Gregorc's Mind Styles traits. A summary of those traits is included in the table below. [2]

Concrete Sequential Thinkers	Abstract Sequential Thinkers
• Are grounded in reality and what they can detect with their senses • Process information in an ordered, linear, and sequential way • Notice details • Recall facts, formulas, and rules easily • Work well with 'hands on' activities broken down into specific tasks • Prefer quiet work environments	• Enjoy theory, abstract thought, and concepts • Analyze information • Are logical, rational, and intellectual • Can focus on what is important (e.g., significant points and details) • Enjoy reading and thoughtful research • Prefer to work alone • Prefer highly structured environments
Concrete Random Thinkers	**Abstract Random Thinkers**
• Are experimental • Are grounded in reality, but take a trial and error approach • Act intuitively to encourage creative thought • Find alternatives and need to do things their own way • Enjoy change • Work well with problem solving activities, but need clear deadlines • Work well with people who value divergent thinking	• Organize ideas, information, and impressions through reflection • Look at the "big picture" first • Thrive in unstructured and people-oriented environments • Believe the real world is based in emotions • Work well with people • Feel constricted in structured environments • Learn by association and visual cues • Need to leave plenty of time to complete a task

With learning styles inventory information, students will have a better understanding of themselves as well as their group members. Collaborative groups can better determine individual member strengths and assign tasks based on those strengths. For example, a strong visual learning group member might be assigned the visual aid task of an assessment. A concrete random thinker may work on the problem solving portion of an assessment. An abstract sequential thinker may conduct the research portion of an assessment. Collaborative group members could proactively plan and compromise to avoid conflict if members have polar opposite learning styles like concrete sequential and abstract random. Student learning styles inventory information is quite useful for a teacher to plan lessons and differentiate instruction as well.

Communication

If we tell students they need to be good communicators, we run the risk of being overly general. Students may struggle with what being a good communicator means. The more clearly we can define good communication, the better the chances are that our students will become good communicators. To help students break down its observable components, good communication is divided into three main categories in the *Collaborative Group Rubric*: verbal communication, non-verbal communication, and active listening.

Speaking clearly, concisely, and persuasively, checking for understanding and agreement, being tactful yet assertive, reasoning logically, providing helpful and constructive feedback, encouraging group members, using effective volume and tone, and addressing group members by name all comprise favorable verbal communication. Smiling, nodding, leaning forward, maintaining good eye contact, facing a speaker, and keeping arms uncrossed all convey positive non-verbal communication. Active listening techniques include: listening for understanding, paraphrasing and reflecting a speaker's comments, asking meaningful questions for clarity, exhibiting empathy, and encouraging a speaker.

Team Work

Similarly, if we tell our students they need to be good team players, we run the risk of being overly general. We must clearly define what we mean by good team work. In the *Collaborative Group Rubric*, Team Work means all group members:

- work toward a uniform goal,
- equally participate,
- consistently share information and ideas,
- give and seek input,
- welcome unique perspectives,
- demonstrate flexibility,
- praise each member's contributions, and
- consistently exhibit courtesy (e.g., consult with group members and notify the group of changes in a timely manner, help group members).

It may help students to visualize how players on a sports team work together to win a game or match. While each team player may have an individual role, the team must work together and assist each other to achieve their ultimate goal: winning the game. That is how students should behave in collaborative groups. While they may be responsible for their individual tasks, team members must work together and assist each other to achieve their ultimate goal: a quality academic product.

Problem Solving

If designed effectively, there are two types of problems students will likely solve in collaborative groups. Ideally, the discipline specific content needed to complete a collaborative group assessment will require students to problem solve. For example, given the ongoing conflict between Israelis and Palestinians, collaborative groups in a social studies class could be asked to determine what actions, if any, the president should take to mediate the conflict. Students would be required to justify their recommendation. Inquiry-based problem solving, either teacher or student generated, is recommended.

In an environmental science class, collaborative groups could be asked to determine what forms of renewable energy the United States should invest in to promote environmental preservation and energy independence. Again, students would be required to justify their selections. In both instances, collaborative groups are engaged in high-level, inquiry-based problem solving that requires a thorough understanding of discipline specific content. Real world-based assessments like these encourage students to use knowledge and content to develop practical problem solving skills.

When students work collaboratively, group-related issues inevitably arise that require problem solving skills. It is likely that this is the second type of problem solving students will be engaged in. The Problem Solving division of the *Collaborative Group Rubric* accounts for these issues as well and further identifies Problem Solving as creatively overcoming obstacles or unexpected circumstances and utilizing conflict resolution methods. Conflict resolution methods are defined as:

- remaining positive,
- tactfully giving timely feedback that defines a problem and negotiates a solution,
- avoiding criticism,
- using "I" language instead of "you" language, and
- understanding a group member's perspective.

Professionalism

Given so many current employers and managers identify a lack of professionalism in young workers, adding a Professionalism component to the *Collaborative Group Rubric* is important. Key aspects of Professionalism include:

- maintaining and encouraging positive, respectful, and open-minded interactions,
- exhibiting equal partnership and a strong work ethic,
- demonstrating professional speech and dress,
- remaining focused, and
- avoiding technological or other distractions.

I will not allow my students to be distracted by their personal devices in class. If I learned one of my students sent a text message or answered a phone call during a job interview (let alone brought a mother or father along), I would feel like I failed as an educator. Failed miserably. If Millennials are unaware of what constitutes professional behavior, it is our job as educators to teach them.

Invest the Time to Break Down the Collaborative Group Rubric at the Start

Taking the time to help students understand the *Collaborative Group Rubric* when it is first introduced is an investment worth making. Talking to students about their previous positive and negative group experiences is important. In those discussions students will likely touch upon some of the areas identified in the rubric and natural connections to the rubric can be made. Students will be more likely to see the value in practicing the soft skills the rubric encourages if they can make connections to their past experiences. My students welcomed the opportunity to talk about their past group experiences. Discussing each of the five rubric components with students is important to clearly define collaborative group behavior expectations. Students have a better chance of successfully developing their soft skills if they know what soft skill behavior is expected of them. Students can even role-play good verses poor verbal communication or non-verbal communication with a partner. Similarly, students can give examples of effective team work. Sample resources and activities to help students practice each of the five rubric components are included in Chapter 5.

I realize time is a limited commodity in education and asking teachers to take class time to teach students soft skills is asking a great deal. We hardly have enough time to get through our curriculum or to allow our students to thoroughly practice important hard skills. We feel it even more when we infuse state and federal initiatives. Increased student assessments are required to meet new teacher evaluation requirements. Some days we feel like jugglers with an endless supply of balls being thrown our way. However, a little time carefully invested in the beginning will yield quality student products in the end, not to mention a likely reduction in student conflict overall. When strong soft skill students populate the classrooms and hallways of our schools, our schools become better places. School culture will likely improve and incidences of bullying and violence will likely decrease. Investing time in our students' soft skill development is a sound investment.

How to Use the Collaborative Group Rubric with Your Existing Assessments

The *Collaborative Group Rubric* is meant to be a practical assessment tool for teachers and students. It can be used with group activities and assessments teachers have previously created in one of two ways: 1. The rubric score can be added as a point value component to an already existing assessment; or 2. The rubric score can exist as a stand-alone grade.

Method 1: Adding the Collaborative Group Rubric to an Existing Assessment

The Mock House Judiciary Impeachment Hearing of FDR assessment that follows exemplifies this first method. The *Collaborative Group Rubric* is valued at 20 points and is added to the already existing assignment. Previously, the assignment had five assessed areas, worth a total of 80 points (See Mock House Judiciary Impeachment Hearing of FDR Assessment List 1). The *Collaborative Group Rubric* was added as a sixth assessed area "6. Collaborative group demonstrated effective project management, communication, teamwork, problem solving, and professionalism (see *Collaborative Group Rubric*)" and valued at 20 points in the Mock House Judiciary Impeachment Hearing of FDR Assessment List 2. The previously 80 point valued Mock House Judiciary Impeachment Hearing of FDR Assessment List 1, with the added 20 point *Collaborative Group Rubric* score, will now be worth 100 points in the second assessment. The collaborative group's performance on the rubric will need to be converted to a score out of 20 points. Please refer to *Table 1: Converting Collaborative Group Rubric to Grade Equivalent Scores* later in the chapter for conversion details.

Mock House Judiciary Impeachment Hearing of FDR

Background: Franklin Delano Roosevelt received many accolades for his initial relief, recovery, and reform efforts during the Great Depression. However, some questioned whether he overstepped his presidential authority as delineated in the United States Constitution. In March 1939 United States special prosecutor George B. Harvey and his legal team are called to testify before the House Judiciary Committee because the committee is considering recommending FDR be impeached under the following articles of impeachment: 1. Violating the system of checks and balances as set forth in Articles I, II, and II of the U.S. Constitution; and 2. Assuming dictatorial powers under the false pretense of economic necessity, while not solving the nation's economic troubles. Harvey has been investigating President Roosevelt for the past year and strongly believes Roosevelt has violated the Constitution and should be removed from office. President Roosevelt's legal team will present to the House Judiciary hearing as well.

Task: You, along with your collaborative group members, will participate in the House Judiciary impeachment hearing taking on one of the following roles: House Judiciary Committee member, George B. Harvey and prosecution legal team, or President Roosevelt's legal defense team. In order to take on your assigned role, your group must research the powers of the President, Congress, and the Supreme Court as delineated in Articles I, II, and II of the U.S. Constitution *and* Roosevelt's actions during the Great Depression. Pay close attention to the constitutionality of Roosevelt's actions and his relationship with Congress and the Supreme Court. Each legal team will be given 20 minutes to present its case and the House Judiciary Committee may interject with questions at any time. After legal team presentations, the House Judiciary Committee will convene, analyze the evidence presented, and vote on each article of impeachment. The House Judiciary Committee will present its articles of impeachment decision and rationale. Each collaborative group must submit an annotative bibliography using proper MLA format and consisting of a minimum of five reliable sources.

Mock House Judiciary Impeachment Hearing of FDR Assessment List 1

(Without the *Collaborative Group Rubric* Score)

Assessed Area	Possible Points	Points Earned Student	Teacher
1. Collaborative group showed accurate and thorough understanding of Articles I, II, and III of the Constitution.	20	_____	_____
2. Collaborative group showed accurate and thorough understanding of FDR's actions and relationship with Congress and the Supreme Court during the Great Depression.	20	_____	_____
3. Collaborative group's presentation showed sound reasoning and strong critical thinking skills.	20	_____	_____
4. Collaborative group used class time effectively.	10	_____	_____
5. Annotated bibliography contains a minimum of five reliable sources and adheres to proper MLA format.	10	_____	_____
TOTAL POINTS EARNED:		_____	_____

Mock House Judiciary Impeachment Hearing of FDR Assessment List 2
(With the added *Collaborative Group Rubric* Score)

Assessed Area	Possible Points	Points Earned Student	Teacher
1. Collaborative group showed accurate and thorough understanding of Articles I, II, and III of the Constitution.	20	_____	_____
2. Collaborative group showed accurate and thorough understanding of FDR's actions and relationship with Congress and the Supreme Court during the Great Depression.	20	_____	_____
3. Collaborative group's presentation showed sound reasoning and strong critical thinking skills.	20	_____	_____
4. Collaborative group used class time effectively.	10	_____	_____
5. Annotated bibliography contains a minimum of five reliable sources and adheres to proper MLA format.	10	_____	_____
6. Collaborative group demonstrated effective project management, communication, teamwork, problem solving, and professionalism (see *Collaborative Group Rubric*).	**20**	_____	_____
TOTAL POINTS EARNED:		_____	_____

Method 2: Using the Collaborative Group Rubric as a Stand Alone Grade

The second method of incorporating the *Collaborative Group Rubric* in student grades is to convert the rubric score to a separate, stand-alone grade. For teachers who have already created effective collaborative group assessments, this may be the easiest way to incorporate the *Collaborative Group Rubric* while supporting students in their soft skill development. It is recommended that the grade be a minimum of 20 points, or equal to 20% of a project grade, so students understand how they work in collaborative groups reasonably contributes toward their grade. Students receive this collaborative group grade *in addition* to the content grade for an assessment.

Converting Collaborative Group Rubric Numeric Score to a Grade

It is important to note that although there are five criterion areas of the *Collaborative Group Rubric* (Project Management, Communication, Team Work, Problem Solving, and Professionalism) and the rubric has four point levels (4-Exemplary, 3-Proficient, 2-Basic, and 1-Below Basic), teachers should not simply add the points for each criterion area to determine a student's score out of 20 points. If a teacher does this, a student will most often receive a numeric score that does not accurately reflect the student's performance. For example, if a student receives a Proficient-3 in Project Management, a Proficient-3 in Communication, a Proficient-3 in Team Work, a Proficient-3 in Problem Solving, and a Proficient-3 in Professionalism, if simply added the student's rubric score would 15. Fifteen out of 20 points is equivalent to a 75%, or C range score. The Proficient descriptors indicate performance well above a C range grade, so simply adding the rubric criterion numbers would not accurately reflect the student's performance.

In general, 4-Exemplary scores should translate to an A range grade, 3-Proficient scores should translate to a B range grade, 2-Basic scores should translate to a C range grade, and 1-Below Basic scores should translate to a D to F range grade.

Collaborative Group Rubric Score	Grade Equivalent Score
4-Exemplary	A range (90-100)
3-Proficient	B range (80-89)
2-Basic	C range (70-79)
1-Below Basic	D to F range (69 and below)

It is recommended that students receive a collaborative group score that counts for a minimum of 20% of an overall project grade. Then students will understand that effective group collaboration reasonably contributes toward their final grade. At the same time, the majority of their final grade is based on content knowledge and analysis. In other words, student grades are 20% soft skills based and 80% hard skills based. This is a reasonable soft skill/hard skill grade ratio. *Table 1: Converting Collaborative Group Rubric to Grade Equivalent Scores*, located on the following page, will help teachers convert rubric number scores to grade equivalent scores out of a 20 point value.

Table 1: Converting *Collaborative Group Rubric* to Grade Equivalent Scores

Letter Grade Range	Collaborative Group Rubric Score	Grade Equivalent Score out of 20 Points
A+	20	20
A	19	19
A-	17-18	18
B+	16	17 or 17.5
B	15	17
B-	13-14	16
C+	11-12	15 or 15.5
C	10	15
C-	9	14
D+	8	13 or 13.5
D	7	13
D-	6	12
F	5	11 and below

Collaborative Group Rubric

Criterion	4-Exemplary	3-Proficient	2-Basic	1-Below Standard
Project Management	•Thoroughly determines a project organizational structure (e.g., efficiently shares contact information, effectively decides meeting schedule, communication methods, how group decisions will be made, group members roles, and how work will be monitored in a manner pleasing to all group members) • Skillfully analyzes project tasks, prioritizes tasks, and distributes tasks fairly based on group member strengths	•Competently determines a project organizational structure (e.g., shares contact information, decides meeting schedule, communication methods, how group decisions will be made, group members roles, and how work will be monitored) •Logically analyzes project tasks, prioritizes tasks, and equally distributes tasks among group members	•Satisfactorily determines a basic project organizational structure (e.g., shares most contact information, partially decides meeting schedule, communication methods, how group decisions will be made, group members roles, and how work will be monitored) •Analyzes most project tasks, somewhat prioritizes tasks, and may unequally distribute tasks among group members	•Ineffectively determines a project organizational structure (e.g., inadequately shares contact information, does not adequately decide meeting schedule, communication methods, how group decisions will be made, group members roles, and how work will be monitored) •Project analysis omits key tasks, inaccurately prioritizes tasks, and unequally distributes tasks among group members
Communication	•Skillfully demonstrates effective **verbal communication** (e.g., speaks clearly, concisely and persuasively, checks for understanding and agreement, is tactful and assertive, reasons logically, provides helpful constructive feedback, encourages group members, uses effective volume and tone, addresses group members by name) • Skillfully demonstrates effective **non-verbal communication** (e.g., consistently smiles, nods, leans forward, maintains good eye contact, faces speaker, keeps arms uncrossed) •Effectively uses **active listening** techniques (e.g. listens for understanding, paraphrases and reflects on speaker's comments, asks meaningful questions for clarity, exhibits empathy, encourages speaker)	•Competently demonstrates effective **verbal communication** (e.g., speaks clearly and concisely, checks for understanding and agreement, is tactful and assertive, reasons logically, provides constructive feedback, uses appropriate volume and tone, addresses group members by name) •Competently demonstrates effective **non-verbal communication** (e.g., often smiles, leans forward, maintains good eye contact, faces speaker, keeps arms uncrossed) •Uses **active listening** techniques (e.g. listens for understanding, paraphrases and summarizes speaker's comments, asks questions for clarity, exhibits some empathy)	•Adequately demonstrates acceptable **verbal communication** (e.g., mostly speaks clearly and concisely, sometimes checks for understanding and is tactful, attempts logical reasoning, attempts constructive feedback, uses acceptable volume and tone, sometimes addresses group members by name) •Demonstrates acceptable **non-verbal communication** (e.g., sometimes maintains good eye contact, faces speaker, keeps arms uncrossed) •Attempts the use of **active listening** techniques (e.g. tries to listen for understanding and to paraphrase speaker's comments)	•Demonstrates ineffective **verbal communication** (e.g., rarely speaks clearly and concisely, rarely checks for understanding or agreement, lacks tact and is aggressive or passive, reasons illogically, feedback is not constructive, uses ineffective volume and tone, rarely addresses group members by name) •Demonstrates ineffective **non-verbal communication** (e.g., does not maintain good eye contact, rarely faces speaker, head is down, keeps arms crossed) •Does not use **active listening** techniques and often listens simply to respond

Criterion	4-Exemplary	3-Proficient	2-Basic	1-Below Standard
Team Work	•All team members cohesively work toward a uniform goal, equally participate in partnership, consistently share information and ideas, and give and seek input •Welcomes unique perspectives, consistently demonstrates flexibility, and praises each member's contributions •Consistently exhibits courtesy (e.g., consults with team and notifies team of changes in a timely fashion, routinely helps teammates)	•All team members work toward a uniform goal, equally participate, share information and ideas, and give and seek input •Recognizes each member has a valid perspective, demonstrates flexibility, and acknowledges individual contributions •Exhibits courtesy (e.g., notifies team of changes, helps teammates when individual tasks are complete)	•Team members complete individual tasks independently, sometimes share information and ideas, and occasionally give and seek input •May recognize each member's perspective and inconsistently demonstrates flexibility •Exhibits moderate courtesy and occasionally helps teammates	•Some team members complete individual tasks, information, input, and ideas are shared minimally •Unaccepting of each member's perspective and inflexible •Lack s courtesy and little to no assistance is given to teammates
Problem Solving	•Insightfully addresses all problem-solving content of the assignment •Creatively overcomes obstacles or unexpected circumstances •Effectively utilizes **conflict resolution** methods (e.g., remains positive, tactfully gives timely feedback that defines a problem and negotiates a solution, avoids criticism, uses "I" language, considers and understands another perspective)	•Sufficiently addresses all problem-solving content of the assignment •Overcomes most obstacles or unexpected circumstances •Utilizes **conflict resolution** methods (e.g., remains positive, tactfully gives feedback that defines a problem and focuses on a solution, avoids criticism, uses "I" language, willing to consider another perspective)	•Addresses most problem-solving content of the assignment •Attempts to overcome obstacles or unexpected circumstances •Utilizes few **conflict resolution** methods when encountering problems with group dynamics	•Insufficiently addresses the problem-solving content of the assignment •Little attempt is made to overcome obstacles or unexpected circumstances •Fails to utilize **conflict resolution** methods when encountering problems with group dynamics
Professionalism	•Maintains and encourages positive, respectful, and open-minded interactions •Exhibits equal participation and exceptional work ethic •Thoroughly demonstrates professional speech and dress •Remains completely focused and is not distracted by technology or other stimuli	•Maintains positive and respectful interactions •Exhibits equal participation and a strong work ethic •Demonstrates professional speech and dress •Remains focused and is not distracted by technology or other stimuli	•Maintains some positive and respectful interactions •Exhibits imbalanced participation with inconsistent work ethic •Mostly demonstrates professional speech and dress •Usually focused and is not often distracted by technology or other stimuli	•Fails to interact in a positive, respectful, and accepting manner •Inadequate participation and work ethic is lacking •Demonstrates unprofessional speech or dress •Lacks focus and is distracted by technology and other stimuli

CHAPTER 5

Resources and Activities to Support Student Soft Skill Development: Grades 6-12

The *Collaborative Group Rubric* identifies and measures the soft skills middle and high school students need for success in school and the workplace. However, if teachers simply hand students the rubric and review its contents, it is unlikely that sufficient soft skill support will occur. Students must clearly define and practice soft skills *prior* to engaging in collaborative group projects and *during* collaborative group work. Teachers need to support soft skill development before, during, and after collaborative group projects.

Resources and activities for each of the five *Collaborative Group Rubric* areas are included in this chapter to provide middle and high school students with the opportunity to practice and develop soft skills before and during collaborative group projects. Teachers are encouraged to take the time to pre-teach soft skills prior to students engaging in the academic content of collaborative group projects. As students become more familiar with the *Collaborative Group Rubric* and more proficiently develop soft skills, front-loading soft skills will no longer be necessary.

Project Management

Effective Project Management is the foundation for which the entire collaborative group project is built. Therefore, giving students class time to develop a *Project Management Plan* is essential. Students should determine a project organizational structure as well as analyze, prioritize, and distribute project tasks. A sample *Project Management Plan* is provided on the following pages. Collaborative group members should complete the *Project Management Plan* and hand it in for teacher review, support, and feedback. This gives a teacher the opportunity to identify project management concerns in order to provide support to collaborative groups in need, thus reducing the chances of group conflict. If appropriate, collaborative group members can revise their *Project Management Plan* based on teacher feedback. The teacher and the collaborative group should retain a copy of the *Project Management Plan* or the plans should be stored in a central location of the classroom to give students the opportunity to refer back to their plan for the duration of the collaborative group project.

Project Management Plan

Collaborative Group Member Names:

_____   _____

_____   _____

We, the above listed collaborative group members, agree to adhere to the following Project Management Plan:

Decision-Making

Collaborative group decisions will be made by:

_____Majority rule

_____Consensus

_____Other (Explain other method)_____

Contact Information

In order to communicate outside of class, we have exchanged contact information and have agreed to communicate in the following ways (check all that apply):

_____In-person meetings   _____Emails   _____Texts

_____Phone conversations   _____Social Media   _____Video Conferencing

_____Other (Explain)_____

Meeting Schedule:

In addition to meeting during class time, we agree to the following communication/meeting schedule:

Date   Time   Date   Time

_____   _____   _____   _____

_____   _____   _____   _____

_____   _____   _____   _____

Task Analysis:

In order to meet the requirements of the project, the following tasks must be completed:

_____   _____

_____   _____

_____   _____

_____   _____

_____   _____

_____   _____

Prioritizing and Assigning Tasks:

Rank the order in which tasks should be completed based on importance and their connection to other tasks. Assign collaborative group members tasks and give a *brief* reason why members were assigned each task.

Task	Group Member(s)	Reason
1.		
2.		
3.		
4.		
5.		
6.		
7.		
8.		
9.		
10.		

Monitoring of Collaborative Group Work:

Briefly explain your plan to monitor collaborative work within your group. How regularly and in what format will collaborative group members report their progress on assigned tasks?

_____

_____

_____

_____

_____

_____

_____

Collaborative Group Member Signatures:

_____   _____

_____   _____

_____

Date

Communication

Good verbal and non-verbal communication is essential, but is often difficult to self-assess. The way we perceive we are communicating may be received quite differently by the person we are communicating with. This is a particular problem for teens that overuse technology and reduce their in-person communication experiences. Communication skills are inhibited when they aren't practiced.

In order to avoid a communication self-perception problem, students should be given the opportunity to practice communicating in pairs for a ten minute time period, with each student leading the communication for four of the ten minutes. Students should be given a prompt to guide their communication. The prompt can be content specific or general in nature. The choice is left to the individual teacher. The purpose of the prompt is to focus the student communication. In a content specific prompt, a science teacher may ask students to identify the most significant scientific discovery of all time. A social studies teacher may ask students to identify the characteristic that best captures the American identity. An English language arts teacher may ask students to change one aspect of the protagonist's character and predict how that might alter the outcome of a novel. Prompts can easily be connected to the compelling question of a unit or class. In a more general prompt, students may be asked to identify the place they would most like to travel to.

Regardless of whether a prompt is content specific or general in nature, students will be expected to give a spoken response to the prompt and *justify* their response within a four minute period. During this time, the speaking student will practice verbal and nonverbal communication and the listening student will pay close attention to this communication. In addition, the listening student will have the opportunity to practice nonverbal communication as well. At the conclusion of the four minutes, the listening student will be allotted one minute to practice active listening techniques. Then the speaking student and the listening student will exchange roles and repeat the exercise.

Ten minutes should be allotted to allow each speaker the opportunity to lead communication for four minutes and each listener to practice active listening techniques for one minute. At the conclusion of the ten minutes, the pair should be given time to assess each other's verbal and non-verbal communication using the *Good Communication Inventory* provided on the following page. Each student will assess his/her partner. Upon receiving an assessment of their communication skills, students can reflect on and choose a communication goal they would like to work on. In the process of assessing each other's communication, students will familiarize themselves with the components of good verbal and nonverbal communication. Ideally, students will internalize these communication components over time if given enough practice and reflection opportunities.

Practice Communication Activity and Time Break-Down

Student 1(Speaker): Leads communication by responding to teacher-generated prompt	4 Minutes
Student 2: Practices active listening techniques by paraphrasing, asking questions, etc.	1 Minute
Student 2(Speaker): Leads communication by responding to teacher-generated prompt	4 Minutes
Student 1: Practices active listening techniques by paraphrasing, asking questions, etc.	1 Minute

Good Communication Inventory

Speaker:

Assessor/Active Listener:

Directions: Please circle the rating number that best describes the speaker's verbal and nonverbal communication.

	Always	Sometimes	Rarely	Never
A. Speaks clearly and concisely.	4	3	2	1
B. Speaks persuasively and logically.	4	3	2	1
C. Checks for understanding/agreement.	4	3	2	1
D. Is tactful and assertive.	4	3	2	1
E. Uses effective volume and tone.	4	3	2	1
F. Maintains good eye contact, smiles/nods.	4	3	2	1
G. Leans forward with arms uncrossed.	4	3	2	1
H. Listens to understand.	4	3	2	1
I. Paraphrases/reflects when listening.	4	3	2	1
J. Encouraging/empathetic when listening.	4	3	2	1

Team Work

While many students can sufficiently complete the components of a group project, few students truly collaborate when completing group projects. Instead, students divide project tasks, complete the tasks individually, and piece the tasks together at the last minute with little comprehension of how the tasks fit together for an overall, big picture understanding of the project. It is as if the tasks are fabric patches and there is no common thread that binds them. If the group project culminates with an in-class presentation and one group member is absent, often the remaining group members have little to no understanding of the absent member's task content. In a situation like this, group members often state "We don't know that. That was Madison's part," in the midst of the class presentation. Group members generally seem confused when I explain the entirety of the project is the responsibility of *all* group members.

Often collaborative group projects are intended to encourage active student engagement. Instead, in situations like these, group projects are encouraging less student accountability and reducing the amount of content information students are exploring. These are unintended consequences of group projects and can be remedied. Setting a clear expectation that *all* collaborative group members are responsible for the *entirety* of a final project product is important at the onset of a collaborative group project. Statements like "That was so and so's part," will not excuse incomplete project components. Additionally, students must be made aware that while it is acceptable for students to divide project tasks among group members, the expectation is that these completed tasks will be pieced together collaboratively for a greater understanding of the project as a whole. All group members will be held accountable for demonstrating the overall, big picture understanding of the project. Surely, teachers don't create collaborative group projects to diminish students' depth of content understanding and exploration. Students need to be aware of this.

The expectation that students are to work as a team to accomplish a uniform project goal must be established at the onset of a collaborative group project. To assist students in creating a uniform collaborative group project goal and to encourage students to work together as a team, I recommend having students complete the *Team Work Collaborative Group Assessment* located on the following pages. Students should identify the collaborative group goal in Section 1 when they complete their *Project Management Plan, prior* to beginning the academic content work of a collaborative group project. Doing this will reinforce the idea that students are expected to work toward one, uniform group goal rather than divide and independently complete individual project tasks.

The *Team Work Collaborative Group Assessment* requires collaborative group members to assess their group's demonstration of key team work skills, including: equally participating as partners, consistently sharing information and ideas, giving and seeking input, being open to unique perspectives, demonstrating flexibility, praising member's contributions, and exhibiting courtesy. Section 2 of the *Team Work Collaborative Group Assessment* should be completed by the collaborative group in the *middle* of the project. One *Team Work Collaborative Group Assessment* will be completed by the collaborative group and handed in to the teacher. The teacher should not look at the collaborative group's assessment scores in a cursory manner, but rather evaluate how the collaborative group reflected on its team work performance. A ten point value score could be given to the *Team Work*

Collaborative Group Assessment to further encourage a collaborative group's reflection. Collaborative groups that show genuine reflection could be given a score of ten out of ten points, while groups showing moderate reflection may receive a score of seven out of ten points. Collaborative groups showing limited reflection may receive a score of three out of ten points.

Having students complete the *Team Work Collaborative Group Assessment* in the middle of the collaborative group project is deliberate and important. While encouraging reflection and reminding students what important team work skills are, completing the *Team Work Collaborative Group Assessment* in the middle of a project allows a collaborative group to identify team work weakness areas and improve on them *prior* to the conclusion of the collaborative group project. This supports students in the development of team work skills and increases their chances of optimal performance on the collaborative group project.

Team Work Collaborative Group Assessment

Collaborative Group Member Names:

_____   _____

_____   _____

Section 1

Collaborative Group Goal: (Complete at the **beginning** of the collaborative group project)

_____

_____

_____

_____

_____

_____

_____

Section 2

Assessment Directions: Please circle the rating number that best describes your level of professionalism in the following areas: (Complete in **middle** of collaborative group project)

	Always	Sometimes	Rarely	Never
A. Works cohesively toward a uniform goal.	4	3	2	1
B. Equally participates in partnership.	4	3	2	1
C. Shares information and ideas.	4	3	2	1
D. Gives and seeks input.	4	3	2	1
E. Welcomes unique perspectives.	4	3	2	1
F. Praises member's contributions.	4	3	2	1
G. Notifies of changes in a timely fashion.	4	3	2	1
H. Routinely helps teammates.	4	3	2	1

Collaborative Group Reflection: (Complete in **middle** of collaborative group project)

Based on our collaborative group's assessment ratings, we would like to improve in the following team work areas: _____

_____

The actions we will take as a collaborative group to improve in these team work areas include:

_____

_____

_____

_____

Problem Solving

Given inevitable group-related issues tend to arise when students work collaboratively, teachers should encourage students to use conflict resolution skills to trouble-shoot these issues. If possible, students can proactively plan to prevent some group-related issues from occurring in the first place. For example, if students completed learning styles inventories prior to engaging in collaborative group work, students can distribute tasks that most closely align with group member strengths. A concrete-sequential learner might be assigned a timeline component of a collaborative group project. A kinesthetic learner might build a model to visually represent the collaborative group's ideas. Likewise, assigning a task that requires a group member to utilize his learning style weakness could cause frustration, delay task completion, and prevent the collaborative group from moving forward as a team toward their goal of successful project completion. For example, it would not benefit the collaborative group to assign a group member with a relative auditory learning style weakness the task of listening to audio recordings of speeches to identify how presidents use tone and imagery to impact public opinion.

Even if students do not have access to learning styles inventory data, giving students the opportunity to practice conflict resolution methods *prior* to engaging in collaborative group activities can give students the tools they need to deal with difficulties that arise within their collaborative groups. Sample practice problem-solving scenarios are included. Students can independently determine how they would resolve each scenario conflict and responses can be shared and evaluated in either small group or whole class discussions.

Problem Solving Scenario #1

Scenario: You are working in a collaborative group that has been given two weeks to research and determine which renewable energy source is best to promote American energy independence. You are required to present and justify your choice to the class in a ten minute presentation. As a collaborative group, you decided that each group member will spend four days researching the benefits and liabilities of one assigned renewable energy source option. On the fifth day, after research is completed individually, collaborative group members will discuss the benefits and liabilities of each renewable energy source so the group can decide which energy option is best for America. The remaining days allocated for the project would be spent planning and preparing the in-class presentation as a group. When the group meets on day five, three group members are prepared to share their research and one group member is unprepared. The unprepared group member states a family matter prevented her from completing her portion of the research.

Directions: Write a response to each question below. Be prepared to share your responses and your reasoning with the class.

1. *How do you propose resolving this collaborative group problem? Be specific in what you would say and what actions you would take.*
2. *What could have been done to prevent this collaborative group problem from occurring? Be specific in your response.*

Problem Solving Scenario #2

<u>Scenario:</u> Your collaborative group and other groups in the class have been asked to answer the following question: "What does it mean to be a responsible global citizen in the twenty-first century?" Collaborative groups must present their answer and rationale to the class in a five minute presentation. Groups can present their answers and rationales in a format of their choosing. One group decided to create a painting. Another group decided to write a song. Some groups have chosen the more traditional PowerPoint or Prezi presentation route. Your collaborative group decided to create a narrative video using a movie-making software program. Your collaborative group needs to select approximately 100 photographs to use in the video before the recorded voice-over narrative can be embedded. On the first day of the project, your collaborative group brainstormed ideas and agreed on a definition of a responsible twenty-first century global citizen. Your group decided that two collaborative group members will write the script and record the voice-over narrative, while the remaining two group members find and save photographs that capture the group-determined definition. When the collaborative group meets to create their movie by combining the recorded audio narrative and selected photographs, the pair responsible for photographs realizes the flash drive containing their 100 photographs is missing. The project is due the next morning.

<u>Directions for Problem Solving Scenario #2:</u> Write a response to each question below. Be prepared to share your responses and your reasoning with the class.

1. *How do you propose resolving this collaborative group problem? Be specific in what you would say and what actions you would take.*

2. *What could have been done to prevent this collaborative group problem from occurring? Be specific in your response.*

Professionalism

Professionalism in collaborative groups consists of: maintaining and encouraging positive, respectful and open-minded interactions, exhibiting equal partnership and a strong work ethic, demonstrating professional speech and dress, and remaining focused. Given students can only control their own professional behaviors and actions, professionalism should be assessed individually within a collaborative group. A *Professionalism Self-Assessment* tool is included to clearly delineate professional behavior. When teachers ask students to complete the *Professionalism Self-Assessment*, they are encouraging students to reflect on their own professional behaviors. Much like the *Team Work Collaborative Group Assessment,* a ten point value score could be given to students when they complete the *Professionalism Self-Assessment.* Students demonstrating genuine reflection could be given a score of ten out of ten points. Students showing moderate reflection may receive a score of seven out of ten points. Students showing limited reflection may receive a score of three out of ten points.

Given a number of Millenials appear at job interviews in unprofessional attire, asking students to dress professionally when participating in class presentations seems logical. Student athletes often dress professionally on days of games, matches, and meets. It seems reasonable to ask students to do the same on days they are presenting to the class. Our students need the practice. However, if district-wide socioeconomic factors inhibit the availability of student professional attire, this request could be omitted.

Professional Self-Assessment

Assessment Directions: Please circle the number that best describes your level of professionalism in the following areas:

		Always	Sometimes	Rarely	Never
A.	I interacted with group members in a positive and respectful manner.	4	3	2	1
B.	I was open to the ideas and suggestions of collaborative group members.	4	3	2	1
C.	I worked hard and acted as an equal partner.	4	3	2	1
D.	I spoke professionally to group members, classmates, and the teacher.	4	3	2	1
E.	I dressed professionally for my class presentation (if applicable).	4	3	2	1
F.	I remained focused and was not distracted by technology or stimuli.	4	3	2	1

CHAPTER 6

Sample Collaborative Group Assessments: Grades 6-12

A number of sample assessments have been included in this chapter to help teachers incorporate collaborative group assessments and the *Collaborative Group Rubric* in their classrooms. The sample assessments encourage student inquiry and are intended to be used with middle and high school students. Students are asked to problem solve and to think critically and creatively. Because I am a social studies teacher, these assessments are based predominantly on social studies content. However, they can easily be adapted to meet the discipline specific content of other subject areas. Famous authors or scientists can be the focus of mock trials in English language arts or science classes. Scientific or mathematical solutions to real-world problems can replace domestic or foreign policy solutions. All assessments are aligned with Common Core and College, Career, and Civics (C3) standards.

Sample Assessment 1: Moonshine Surprise v. United States: Grades 9-12

Compelling Question: *Who should laws protect?*

CCSS-Literacy.RH.9-12.7-Integrate and evaluate multiple sources of information presented in diverse formats and media in order to address a question or solve a problem.

CCSS-ELA.LITERACY.SL.9-12.4-Present information, findings, and supporting evidence clearly, conveying a clear and distinct perspective, such that listeners can follow the line of reasoning, alternative or opposing perspectives are addressed, and the organization, development, substance, and style are appropriate to purpose, audience, and a range of formal and informal tasks.

CCSS-ELA.LITERACY.SL.9-12.5-Make strategic use of digital media (e.g., textual, graphic, audio, visual, and interactive elements) in presentations to enhance understanding of findings, reasoning, and evidence and to add interest.

C3Framework.D1.5-9-12.Determine the kinds of sources that will be helpful in answering compelling and supporting questions, taking into consideration multiple points of view represented in sources, the types of sources available, and the potential use of sources.

C3Framework.D2.His.1.9-12.Evaluate how historical events and developments were shaped by unique circumstances of time and place as well as broader historical contexts.

C3Framework.D2.Civ.4.9-12.Explain how the U.S. Constitution establishes a system of government that has powers, responsibilities, and limits that have changed over time and that are still contested.

<u>C3Framework.D2.Civ.5.9-12.</u>Evaluate citizens' and institutions' effectiveness in addressing social and political problems at the local, state, tribal, national, and/or international level.

<u>C3Framework.D3.1.9-12.</u>Gather relevant information from multiple sources representing a wide range of views while using the origin, authority, structure, context, and corroborative value of the sources to guide the selection.

<u>C3Framework.D4.1.9-12.</u>Construct arguments using precise and knowledgeable claims, with evidence from multiple sources, while acknowledging counterclaims and evidentiary weaknesses.

<u>C3Framework.D4.4.9-12.</u>Critique the use of claims and evidence in arguments for credibility.

<u>Background Information:</u>

The owners of the New Haven-based corporation Moonshine Surprise have been manufacturing their specialized brand of whiskey for years without incident. However, in May of 1915 the U.S. Federal Trade Commission barged onto their premises without warning to inspect their manufacturing facility. After completing an inspection, the Federal Trade Commission closed the Moonshine Surprise manufacturing facility citing the following reasons: 1. The conditions workers, many of whom were children, were subjected to were deplorable (e.g., poor ventilation and lighting, dangerous machinery, long work hours without breaks, low wages); 2. The Moonshine Surprise Corporation was believed to be receiving illegal rebates from the railroad industry to transport whiskey across state lines; and 3. An ingredient in Moonshine Surprise, while currently unregulated by the government, is believed to have hallucinogenic and harmful effects on consumers. The owners of Moonshine Surprise argue that their Fourteenth Amendment rights have been violated because they have been deprived of their right of personal property without due process and their legitimate rights of citizenship have been encroached upon. Additionally, the owners argue, any previous laws passed that support the Federal Trade Commission findings are unconstitutional because they violate the Fourteenth Amendment.

<u>Task:</u> Your task is to determine whether the Fourteenth Amendment rights of the owners of Moonshine Surprise have been violated. Along with collaborative group members, you will take part in a mock U.S. Supreme Court case. Your collaborative group will be assigned one of the following roles:

•U.S. Supreme Court Justices •Lawyers for Moonshine Surprise owners •Lawyers for U.S. government

*Please note, you will graded individually in content areas 1, 2, 3, 5, and 6 and you will be graded as a collaborative group in content area 4.

<u>Purpose:</u>
The purpose of this activity is to evaluate the constitutionality of industrial reforms of the Progressive era, determine the balance between the rights of capital v. the rights labor/individuals, and to analyze various industrial era laws and Supreme Court cases.

Procedure:

1. Review the background information of the Moonshine Surprise case, the Fourteenth Amendment, and the following laws and Supreme Court cases:

Supreme Court Cases: _Munn v. Illinois, Wabash, St. Louis and Pacific Railway Company v. Illinois, Northern Securities Company v. United States,_ and _Danbury Hatters (Loewe v. Lawlor)_

Laws: _Interstate Commerce Act, Sherman Anti-Trust Act, Pure Food and Drug Act, Meat Inspection Act, Railroad Reforms (1903-06), Department of Commerce and Labor, Child Labor Laws, Clayton Anti-Trust Act, Federal Reserve Act,_ and _Federal Trade Act_

2. Lawyers will work collaboratively in groups to prepare cases. Supreme Court Justices will prepare questions for each legal team.

3. Participate in the two day mock Supreme Court trial. Each side will be allotted 30 minutes to present its case, keeping in mind Supreme Court Justices may interject at any time to ask questions. After cases are presented, justices will adjourn to make their decision, and will reconvene to present their opinion(s).

Moonshine Surprise v. United States Assessment List

Content Area	Possible Points	Points Earned Student	Teacher
1. The student used research and class time effectively.	10	_____	_____
2. Student participation in mock Supreme Court activity showed knowledge and understanding of relevant U.S. Supreme Court cases, laws, and the Fourteenth Amendment.	20	_____	_____
3. The student used relevant information from multiple credible sources to build his/her case.	20	_____	_____
4. Collaborative group demonstrated effective project management, communication, teamwork, problem solving, and professionalism (see _Collaborative Group Rubric_).	20	_____	_____
5. The student's participation in mock Supreme Court Activity was persuasive and addresses the compelling question "Who should laws protect?"	20	_____	_____
6. The student's presentation showed reasoning, organization, development, substance, and an understanding of Supreme Court procedure.	10	_____	_____
TOTAL POINTS EARNED:		_____	_____

Sample Assessment 2: LBJ's Advisory Team Written Brief on Vietnam Conflict: Grades 6-12

Compelling Question: *When is war justified?*

CCSS.ELA-Literacy.RH.6-8.1-Cite specific textual evidence to support analysis of primary and secondary sources.

CCSS.ELA-Literacy.RH.6-8.7-Integrate visual information (e.g., in charts, graphs, photographs, videos, or maps) with other information in print and digital texts.

CCSS.ELA-LITERACY.RH.11-12.7-Integrate and evaluate multiple sources of information presented in diverse formats and media in order to address a question or solve a problem.

CCSS.ELA-LITERACY.RH.11-12.9-Integrate information from diverse sources, both primary and secondary, into a coherent understanding of an event, noting discrepancies among sources.

CCSS.ELA-LITERACY.W.7.2-Write informative/explanatory texts to examine a topic and convey ideas, concepts, and information through the selections, organization, and analysis of relevant content.

CCSS.ELA-LITERACY.WHST.11-12.2B-Develop the topic thoroughly by selecting the most significant and relevant facts, extended definitions, concrete details, quotations, or other information and examples appropriate to the audience's knowledge of the topic.

C3Framework.D1.5-6-12.Determine the kinds of sources that will be helpful in answering compelling and supporting questions, taking into consideration multiple points of view represented in sources, the types of sources available, and the potential use of sources.

C3Framework.D2.His.1.6-12.Evaluate how historical events and developments were shaped by unique circumstances of time and place as well as broader historical contexts.

C3Framework.D2.Geo.7.6-12.Analyze the reciprocal nature of how historical events and the spatial diffusion of ideas, technologies, and cultural practices have influenced migration patterns and the distribution of human populations.

C3Framework.D4.1.9-12.Construct arguments using precise and knowledgeable claims, with evidence from multiple sources, while acknowledging counterclaims and evidentiary weaknesses.

C3Framework.D4.4.9-12.Critique the use of claims and evidence in arguments for credibility.

Background: The Vietnam conflict was one of the longest and most unpopular foreign wars in U.S. history. U.S. military involvement began shortly after the country was divided into North and South Vietnam at the Seventeenth Parallel in 1954 when President Eisenhower sent military advisors to aid the South Vietnamese Diem government. In 1962 President Kennedy followed suit and sent an additional 8,000 American troops to "advise" and train the South Vietnamese army. After the 1964 Gulf of Tonkin incident, President Johnson continued to escalate the conflict in Vietnam. In 1966 there were approximately 360,000 American troops in Vietnam, however by 1968 American troop numbers grew to over 700,000. By the war's end nearly 50,000 American soldiers died in the conflict.

A "credibility gap" between the American government and the people about victory in Vietnam grew. While the Vietnam anti-war movement started on a small scale in 1963, in 1965 15% of Americans favored American troop withdrawal from Vietnam. Anti-war sentiments and movements expanded in the U.S., particularly as media coverage exposed the reality of the conflict in Vietnam and events like the My Lai Massacre. Sixty-nine percent of Americans favored U.S. troop withdrawal from Vietnam in 1969 and considered the war a "mistake."

President Johnson personally agonized about the Vietnam conflict, often weeping when signing condolence letters to families of fallen soldiers and privately praying with Catholic monks in Washington D.C. Largely due to the Vietnam conflict President Johnson announced in March 1968 he would not seek a second term as president of the United States. Despite this, President Johnson was deeply committed to victory in Vietnam. The problem was Americans were unsure what victory in Vietnam meant. In May 1968 the North Vietnamese government agreed to attend a peace talk in Paris regarding the conflict.

Task: You, along with three collaborative group members, will be assigned the role one of the following advisors to President Johnson: Secretary of State Dean Rusk, Secretary of Defense Robert McNamara, Attorney General Ramsey Clark, or Vice-President Hubert Humphrey. To prepare President Johnson for the upcoming peace talk, your task is to advise the president what the best option is for the United States in Vietnam. To aid the president you will prepare a written advisory brief as a collaborative team. Your advisory brief must include the following:

1. A definition of victory in Vietnam
2. A list of terms the U.S. is willing to accept in order for a complete withdrawal of American troops from Vietnam
3. A map indicating how Vietnam should be divided (if a division is to exist) at the conclusion of the conflict

LBJ's Advisory Team Written Brief on Vietnam Conflict Assessment List

Content	Possible Points	Points Earned Student	Points Earned Teacher
1. The Advisory Team's definition of victory in Vietnam is convincing, accurately connects to Cold War policies, is developed thoroughly, and answers the compelling question "When is war justified?"	20	_____	_____
2. The list of American terms for withdrawal is logical, reasonable, connects to the definition of victory in Vietnam, and integrates multiple, credible sources.	20	_____	_____
3. The Advisory Team's map accurately portrays the team's terms and shows an understanding of how the Vietnam conflict impacted the distribution of human population.	20	_____	_____
4. Collaborative group demonstrated effective project management, communication, teamwork, problem solving, and professionalism (see *Collaborative Group Rubric*).	20	_____	_____
TOTAL POINTS EARNED:		_____	_____

Sample Assessment 3: Collapse of Communism Symposium: Grades 6-12

Compelling Question: *What role should the U.S. play on the world stage?*

CCSS.ELA-Literacy.RH.6-8.1-Cite specific textual evidence to support analysis of primary and secondary sources.

CCSS.ELA-LITERACY.RH.11-12.7-Integrate and evaluate multiple sources of information presented in diverse formats and media in order to address a question or solve a problem.

CCSS.ELA-LITERACY.RH.11-12.9-Integrate information from diverse sources, both primary and secondary, into a coherent understanding of an event, noting discrepancies among sources.

CCSS.ELA-LITERACY.SL.6-12.1-Initiate and participate in a range of collaborative discussions (one-on-one, in groups, and teacher-led) with diverse partners on grades 6-12 topics, texts, and issues, building on others' ideas and expressing their own clearly and persuasively.

C3Framework.D1.5-6-12.Determine the kinds of sources that will be helpful in answering compelling and supporting questions, taking into consideration multiple points of view represented in sources, the types of sources available, and the potential use of sources.

C3Framework.D2.Hist.1.6-8.Analyze connections among events and developments in broader historical contexts.

C3Framework.D2.His.1.9-12.Evaluate how historical events and developments were shaped by unique circumstances of time and place as well as broader historical contexts.

C3Framework.D2.Eco.8.9-12.Describe the possible consequences, both intended and unintended, of government policies to improve market outcomes.

C3Framework.D3.1.6-12.Gather relevant information from multiple sources representing a wide range of views while using the origin, authority, structure, context, and corroborative value of the sources to guide the selection.

C3Framework.D4.1.6-12.Construct arguments using precise and knowledgeable claims, with evidence from multiple sources, while acknowledging counterclaims and evidentiary weaknesses.

C3Framework.D4.4.6-12.Critique the use of claims and evidence in arguments for credibility.

Background: Post-World War II United States foreign policy was a stark contrast to the previous policy of isolationism. During the Cold War era, containing communism was the driving force behind U.S. foreign policy and caused the U.S. to intervene in numerous nations including: Korea, Iran, Vietnam, Afghanistan, Cuba, and other Latin American countries. When the Cold War ended rather abruptly in 1991 some questioned what would guide U.S. foreign policy.

Task: You, along with collaborative team members, are foreign policy specialists commissioned by the Senate Foreign Relations Committee to attend a Collapse of Communism Symposium in January 1992. Your task is to advise the Senate Foreign Relations Committee as to the future of U.S. foreign policy. Your collaborative group will provide a brief summary of your team's position (in three minutes or less) on what U.S. foreign policy should be in a post-Cold War world and then participate in a dialogue/debate with fellow foreign policy specialists. Your collaborative group must address the following questions:

1. Given the collapse of communism in Eastern Europe and the former Soviet Union, what should the focus of future U.S. foreign policy be?
2. What potential problem(s) does the collapse of communism in Eastern Europe and the former Soviet Union cause? Should the U.S. have a role in solving these problems?

Collapse of Communism Symposium Assessment List

Please note you will be graded individually in content areas 2 and 4 and as a collaborative group in content areas 1 and 3.

Content	Possible Points	Points Earned Student	Points Earned Teacher
1. The collaborative group's summary about the future of U.S. foreign policy was persuasive, logical, had a solid factual foundation, and integrated multiple, credible, and diverse sources. Both task questions are addressed in the summary.	20	_____	_____
2. The student had strong participation in the dialogue/debate about the future of U.S. foreign policy and was attentive and respectful to fellow class foreign policy specialists. The student posed and responded to questions to further overall understanding of the topic and addressed the compelling question "What role should the U.S. play on the world stage?"	20	_____	_____
3. The collaborative group demonstrated effective project management, communication, teamwork, problem solving, and professionalism (see *Collaborative Group Rubric*).	20	_____	_____
4. The student used class and research time effectively, determining the kinds of sources helpful in answering compelling and supporting questions.	10	_____	_____
TOTAL POINTS EARNED:		_____	_____

Sample Assessment 4: African Health Policy Presentations: Grades 6-12

Compelling Question: *What is the purpose of government?*

CCSS.ELA-Literacy.RH.6-8.1-Cite specific textual evidence to support analysis of primary and secondary sources.

CCSS.ELA-LITERACY.RH.11-12.7-Integrate and evaluate multiple sources of information presented in diverse formats and media in order to address a question or solve a problem.

CCSS.ELA-LITERACY.RH.11-12.3-Evaluate various explanations for actions or events and determine which explanation best accords with textual evidence, acknowledging where the text leaves matters uncertain.

CCSS.ELA-LITERACY.RH.11-12.9-Integrate information from diverse sources, both primary and secondary, into a coherent understanding of an idea or event, noting discrepancies among sources.

CCSS.ELA-LITERACY.RH.11-12.1-Cite specific textual evidence to support analysis of primary and secondary sources, connecting insights gained from specific details to an understanding of the text as a whole.

CCSS-LITERACY.SL.6-12.1-Initiate and participate effectively in a range of collaborative discussions with diverse partners on grades 6-12 topics, texts, and issues, building on others' ideas and expressing their own clearly and persuasively.

CCSS-LITERACY.SL.6-12.2-Integrate multiple sources of information presented in diverse formats and media (e.g., visually, quantitatively, orally) in order to make informed decisions and solve problems, evaluating the credibility and accuracy of each source and noting any discrepancies among data.

CCSS-LITERACY.SL.6-12.4-Present information, findings, and supporting evidence clearly, concisely, and logically such that listeners can follow the line of reasoning and the organization, development, substance, and style are appropriate to purpose, audience, and task.

C3Framework.D1.5-6-12.Determine the kinds of sources that will be helpful in answering compelling and supporting questions, taking into consideration multiple points of view represented in sources, the types of sources available, and the potential use of sources.

C3Framework.D2.His.1.6-12.Evaluate how historical events and developments were shaped by unique circumstances of time and place as well as broader historical contexts.

C3Framework.D2.Civ.5.9-12.Evaluate citizens' and institutions' effectiveness in addressing social and political problems at the local, state, tribal, national, and/or international level.

C3Framework.D2.Civ.6.6-8.Describe the roles of political, civic, and economic organizations in shaping people's lives.

C3Framework.D3.1.6-12.Gather relevant information from multiple sources representing a wide range of views while using the origin, authority, structure, context, and corroborative value of the sources to guide the selection.

C3Framework.D4.2.6-12.Construct explanations using sound reasoning, correct sequence (linear or non-linear), examples, and details with significant and pertinent information and data, while acknowledging the strengths and weaknesses of the explanation given its purpose (e.g., cause and effect, chronological, procedural, technical).

Background: Numerous health concerns have plagued African countries. In hopes of better addressing health concerns, many African countries have instituted different governmental health policies that have had varying degrees of success.

Task: In collaborative groups of three, you will research the governmental health policies of an assigned African country. Your research will include:

1. A description of the health concerns of your assigned African country
2. Background of what policies your African government has implemented over the past 30 years to address the health concerns
3. A proposed government policy solution to the health concerns of your African country
4. Benefits of your proposed solution, including an explanation as to why your solution is the BEST solution for your African country's health concerns

Along with your collaborative group members, you will present your research and findings to the class in a 20-25 minute presentation. Your presentation must include the following:

- *a factual account of all research noted in #1-4 above,*
- *an article for students to read <u>prior</u> to the presentation, so your group can facilitate a student-led discussion of the article,*
- *a timeline showing how the African government has dealt with the health issue over the course of 30 years,*
- *an additional visual aid,*
- *a student- led activity for the class to participate in, and*
- *an annotative bibliography consisting of a minimum of <u>seven</u> sources (four must be published sources).*

African Health Policy Presentation Assessment List

Content	Possible Points	Student	Teacher
1. The description of the African health policy issue is accurate and thorough.	10	_____	_____
2. The background of the African health policy issue over the past 30 years is accurate and thorough and a timeline is included.	10	_____	_____
3. The proposed solution to the African health policy issue and justification are logical, contain pertinent information and data, show solid critical thinking skills, and integrate relevant information from multiple, credible sources.	20	_____	_____
4. The annotated bibliography is in proper MLA format and includes a minimum of seven sources (four of the seven must be published sources).	5	_____	_____
5. The group selected article and student-led discussion enhance student understanding of the African health policy issue and connect to the compelling question "What is the purpose of government?"	10	_____	_____
6. The visual aid enhances student understanding of the African health policy issue and shows solid effort.	5	_____	_____
7. The student-led activity engages students and enhances student understanding of the African health policy issue.	10	_____	_____
8. The collaborative group demonstrated effective project management, communication, teamwork, problem solving, and professionalism (see *Collaborative Group Rubric*).	20	_____	_____
9. The group showed solid speaking, listening, and presentation skills.	10	_____	_____
TOTAL POINTS EARNED:		_____	_____

Sample Assessment 5: Written Advisory Brief on the Middle East: Grades 9-12

<u>Compelling Question:</u> *Is world peace possible?*

<u>CCSS-Literacy.WHST.9-12.4</u>-Produce clear and coherent writing in which the development, organization, and style are appropriate to task, purpose, and audience.

<u>CCSS-Literacy.WHST.9-12.7</u>-Conduct short as well as more sustained research projects to answer a question or solve a problem; narrow or broaden the inquiry when appropriate; synthesize multiple sources on the subject, demonstrating understanding of the subject under investigation.

<u>C3Framemwork.D1.1.9-12.</u> Explain how a question reflects an enduring issue in the field.

<u>C3Framework.D1.5-9-12.</u>Determine the kinds of sources that will be helpful in answering compelling and supporting questions, taking into consideration multiple points of view represented in sources, the types of sources available, and the potential use of sources.

<u>C3Framework.D2.His.1.9-12.</u>Evaluate how historical events and developments were shaped by unique circumstances of time and place as well as broader historical contexts.

<u>C3Framework.D3.1.9-12.</u>Gather relevant information from multiple sources representing a wide range of views while using the origin, authority, structure, context, and corroborative value of the sources to guide the selection.

<u>C3Framework.D4.1.9-12.</u>Construct arguments using precise and knowledgeable claims, with evidence from multiple sources, while acknowledging counterclaims and evidentiary weaknesses.

Background: The United States has long been embroiled in Middle East conflict. The terms of the Treaty of Versailles ending World War I divided the Ottoman Empire into mandate nations subject to European influence. Although Middle Eastern mandates eventually gained independence, tension in the Middle East remained. The establishment of the nation of Israel, with a recommended partition plan for Palestinians and Jews at the conclusion of World War II, created long-standing tension in the region that remains today. Despite attempts to garner numerous peace agreements between Arabs and Israelis, conflicts between the two groups continue and the U.S. support of Israel isn't viewed favorably by many Arab nations. U.S. involvement in the region, including the 1953 CIA led coup that overthrew Iran's democratically elected leader and installed Muhammad Reza Pahlavi, led to resentment eventually culminating in the Iran Hostage crisis from 1979-1980. When the CIA armed and funded the mujahideen in the 1980s during the Soviet invasion of Afghanistan, it unknowingly encouraged the rise of Osama bin Laden. Although it acted in coalition with United Nations countries, U.S. actions in the Persian Gulf War of 1991 solidified American involvement in a volatile region. While Middle Eastern terrorism existed prior, 9/11 was the ultimate game changer in terrorism. In response, the U.S. unleashed a War on Terror, vowing to seek justice for those that commit terrorist acts and the nations that harbor them. The war in Afghanistan was America's first military response in the War on Terror. The war in Iraq followed and was initiated first over concern about weapons of mass destruction and later to establish a democratic, Saddam Hussein-free Iraq. The Arab Spring ushered in new governments and leaders in the Middle Eastern countries of Tunisia, Libya, Egypt, and Yemen, while encouraging civil uprisings in many countries, including Syria. Iraq, once a developing democracy, presently endures internal conflict that threatens the existence of its democracy. The rise of the Islamic State of Iraq and Syria (ISIS) has further destabilized the region. Unquestionably, the Middle East has been a region of perpetual conflict. The U.S. has involved itself in the region both diplomatically and militarily to promote Cold War policies, secure oil reserves, and combat terrorism. Some feel the United States should stay out of the Middle East and focus on problems at home. Others believe U.S. involvement in the region is vital to ensure American stability and security.

Task: Along with cooperative group members acting as close advisors to the president, you will recommend a U.S. foreign policy course of action in the Middle East. You will submit one written advisory brief from your group to the president. Your written advisory brief must include the following:

1. An _explanation_ of what you believe to be the lessons the United States should have learned from American involvement in the Middle East from 1919 to the present.
2. A _recommendation_ for future U.S. involvement in the Middle East. Your group must justify your recommendation with critical thinking, logic, and connections to your response in #1. Determine when the U.S. should encourage diplomacy and when the U.S should intervene militarily. Ultimately, your collaborative group must address the question "Is world peace possible?"

Written Advisory Brief on the Middle East Assessment List

Content	Possible Points	Points Earned Student	Teacher
1. The explanation of lessons learned from U.S. involvement in the Middle East from 1919 to the present was thorough and shows clear historical thinking.	20	_____	_____
2. The recommendation for U.S. involvement in the Middle East is connected to #1 and shows solid critical thinking and problem solving skills.	20	_____	_____
3. The written advisory brief is clear and coherent, with development, organization, and style appropriate to task.	20	_____	_____
4. Multiple, credible sources were synthesized in the written advisory brief.	20	_____	_____
5. The collaborative group demonstrated effective project management, communication, teamwork, problem solving, and professionalism (see _Collaborative Group Rubric_).	20	_____	_____
TOTAL POINTS EARNED:		_____	_____

Sample Assessment 6: Slavery Debated at a Joint Session of Congress: Grades 6-12

Compelling Question: *Can a divided people share a nation?*

CCSS-Literacy.WHST.6-12.7-Conduct short as well as more sustained research projects to answer a question or solve a problem; narrow or broaden the inquiry when appropriate; synthesize multiple sources on the subject, demonstrating understanding of the subject under investigation.

CCSS-LITERACY.SL.6-12.1-Initiate and participate effectively in a range of collaborative discussions with diverse partners on grades 6-12 topics, texts, and issues, building on others' ideas and expressing their own clearly and persuasively.

CCSS-LITERACY.SL.6-12.4-Present information, findings, and supporting evidence clearly, concisely, and logically such that listeners can follow the line of reasoning and the organization, development, substance, and style are appropriate to purpose, audience, and task.

CCSS-LITERACY.SL.6-12.6-Adapt speech to a variety of contexts and tasks, demonstrating command of formal English when indicated or appropriate.

C3Framework.D1.5-6-12.Determine the kinds of sources that will be helpful in answering compelling and supporting questions, taking into consideration multiple points of view represented in sources, the types of sources available, and the potential use of sources.

C3Framework.D2.His.1.6-12.Evaluate how historical events and developments were shaped by unique circumstances of time and place as well as broader historical contexts.

C3Framework.D2.Civ.5.9-12.Evaluate citizens' and institutions' effectiveness in addressing social and political problems at the local, state, tribal, national, and/or international level.

C3Framework.D3.1.6-12.Gather relevant information from multiple sources representing a wide range of views while using the origin, authority, structure, context, and corroborative value of the sources to guide the selection.

C3Framework.D4.1.6-12.Construct arguments using precise and knowledgeable claims, with evidence from multiple sources, while acknowledging counterclaims and evidentiary weaknesses.

C3Framework.D4.4.6-12.Critique the use of claims and evidence in arguments for credibility.

Background: By the mid-nineteenth century deep-seated tension existed between the North and South. As new territories were added to the United States, questions arose as to whether they would be free or slave states. These tensions erupted to a level that threatened the very existence of the Union itself. Rumors of secession of the southern states and possible war spread quickly after Lincoln was elected president in 1860. President Buchanan, still in office, did not know what to do.

Task: Your collaborative group will consist of two Senators and two Congressmen from an assigned northern or southern state. In hopes of keeping the Union together and avoiding civil war, a special joint session of Congress is being held in November 1860 to discuss the issue of slavery. Your group's state Congressional delegation, along with other state delegations, will recommend a plan to determine how slavery should be handled in new territories. As congressional representatives of your state, your collaborative group will determine an ideal plan regarding the possible existence of slavery in new territories and what your state would be willing to settle for should other members of Congress not support your state's plan. You, along with collaborative group members, must address the question "Can a divided people share a nation?" Collaborate to complete the attached Slavery Recommendation Summary and be prepared to present/defend your recommendations at the joint session of Congress.

Assessment: Your grade will be determined by the assessment list below.

Slavery Debated at a Joint Session of Congress Assessment List

	Possible Points	Points Earned Student	Teacher
1. The group's Slavery Recommendation Summary is thoughtful, logical, and accurately reflects the perspective of the assigned state.	20	_____	_____
2. Student participation in the joint session of Congress is persuasive, effective, and courteous.	20	_____	_____
3. Multiple, credible sources were synthesized in the written recommendation.	20	_____	_____
4. The collaborative group demonstrated effective project management, communication, teamwork, problem solving, and professionalism (see *Collaborative Group Rubric*).	20	_____	_____
TOTAL POINTS EARNED:		_____	_____

Slavery Recommendation Summary

Collaborative Team Representatives_____

State Represented _____

Ideal Plan for State Admittance in New Territories:

Plan Your State Would Be Willing to Settle For:

Why the Issue of Slavery Is Important to Your State:

Sample Assessment 7: Presidential Campaign Commercial: Grades 6-12

Compelling Question: *Who is best-suited to lead the nation?*

CCSS-Literatcy.RH.6-12.7-Integrate and evaluate multiple sources of information presented in diverse formats and media in order to address a question or solve a problem.

CCSS-LITERACY.SL.6-12.4-Present information, findings, and supporting evidence clearly, conveying a clear and distinct perspective, such that listeners can follow the line of reasoning, alternative or opposing perspectives are addressed, and the organization, development, substance, and style are appropriate to purpose, audience, and a range of formal and informal tasks.

CCSS-LITERACY.SL.6-12.5-Make strategic use of digital media (e.g. textual, graphic, audio, visual, and interactive elements) in presentations to enhance understanding of findings, reasoning, and evidence and to add interest.

C3Framework.D1.5-6-12.Determine the kinds of sources that will be helpful in answering compelling and supporting questions, taking into consideration multiple points of view represented in sources, the types of sources available, and the potential use of sources.

C3Framework- D2.Civ.5.9-12.Evaluate citizens' and institutions' effectiveness in addressing social and political problems at the local, state, tribal, national, and/or international level.

C3Framework-D2.Civ.13.6-12.Evaluate public policies in terms of intended and unintended outcomes, and related consequences.

C3Framework.D3.1.6-12.Gather relevant information from multiple sources representing a wide range of views while using the origin, authority, structure, context, and corroborative value of the sources to guide the selection.

C3Framework.D4.1.6-12.Construct arguments using precise and knowledgeable claims, with evidence from multiple sources, while acknowledging counterclaims and evidentiary weaknesses.

C3Framework.D4.4.6-12.Critique the use of claims and evidence in arguments for credibility.

Directions: In collaborative groups, you will create a one to two minute persuasive campaign commercial for a presidential candidate. Class articles/discussions and recent campaign news should be the basis of your commercial. Your commercial must contain a voice or theme true to the candidate's style. A minimum of two campaign platform issues and the candidate's character must be analyzed and interwoven as well. Your commercial should be completed using Windows Movie Maker or an alternative movie-making software program.

Presidential Campaign Commercial Assessment List

Content	Possible Points	Points Earned Student	Teacher
1. The campaign commercial contains a clear voice/theme true to the candidate's style and addresses the compelling question "Who is best-suited to lead the nation?"	20	_____	_____
2. The campaign commercial contains a minimum of two platform issues that reflect the integration and evaluation of multiple sources.	15	_____	_____
3. The candidate's character is effectively interwoven in the commercial.	15	_____	_____
4. The campaign commercial is persuasive and effective, and contains arguments based on precise information/data and multiple, credible sources.	20	_____	_____
5. The collaborative group demonstrated effective project management, communication, teamwork, problem solving, and professionalism (see *Collaborative Group Rubric*).	20	_____	_____
6. The commercial meets the one to two minute requirement and was enhanced by Windows Movie Maker or an alternative movie making software program.	10	_____	_____
TOTAL POINTS EARNED:		_____	_____

CHAPTER 7

Collaborative Group Rubric and Suggested Activities and Assessments: Grades K-5

While building the soft skill development of teens has been the focus of much of this book, nurturing soft skill development in our elementary school children is encouraged. Children are given smartphones and personal devices at younger and younger ages. If teens and adults struggle to regulate their use of technology, it seems unlikely that elementary age children will exercise any more self-control. Elementary age technological overuse and its negative impact seem inevitable. An adapted *Collaborative Group Rubric: Grades K-5* is included in this chapter to support the soft skill development of elementary age children. Additionally, a number of kindergarten through fifth grade sample activities have been included to help teachers incorporate collaborative group assessments in the classroom. The sample activities promote student inquiry and are aligned with Common Core and College, Career, and Civics (C3) standards. Students are encouraged to think critically and to problem solve creatively in the included activities.

Collaborative Group Rubric: Grades K-5

Criterion	3	2	1
Project Management	•Creates agreed upon rules for the group •Chooses how group decisions will be made •Divides project jobs fairly	•Creates some rules for the group •Chooses how some group decisions will be made •Divides project jobs	•Does not create rules for the group •Does not choose how group decisions will be made •Project jobs are divided unfairly
Communication	•Actively participates in group conversations •Asks and answers questions for better understanding •Shares thoughts and ideas regularly •Speaks clearly and addresses group members by name often •Smiles often, makes good eye contact, and keeps arms uncrossed	•Participates in some group conversations •Asks and answers some questions •Expresses some thoughts and ideas •Speaks clearly and addresses some group members by name •Sometimes smiles and makes some eye contact	•Rarely participates in group conversations •Rarely asks and answers questions •Rarely expresses thoughts and ideas •Speaks, but does not address group members by name •Rarely smiles or makes eye contact
Team Work	•All group members work on the project as a team and help each other •Welcomes the ideas of all group members •Compliments group members on their work	•Most group members work on the project as a team and some help each other •Welcomes the ideas of some group member •Compliments some group members on their work	•Some group members work on the project, but rarely help each other •Does not listen to the ideas of group members •Does not compliment group members on their work
Problem Solving	•Creatively completes the project •Is positive and does not criticize group members •Tries to understand the feelings of group members •If group members disagree, tries to find a solution	•Completes the project •Is positive most of the time and does not criticize group members •Tries to understand the feelings of some group members •Does not cause group disagreements	•Completes part of the project •Complains and criticizes group members •Does not try to understand the feelings of group members •Causes group disagreements
Professionalism	•Always follows group rules •Always comes prepared •Always speaks politely •Always pays attention	•Follows group rules •Comes prepared •Speaks politely •Pays attention	•Rarely follows group rules •Rarely comes prepared •Rarely speaks politely •Rarely pays attention

Sample Activity 1: American Democratic Principles Presentation: Grades K-5

Compelling Question: What does it mean to be an American?

CCSS.ELA-LITERACY.RI.K-5.2-Determine two or more main ideas of a text and explain how they are supported by key details; summarize the text.

CCSS.ELA-LITERACY.RI.K-5.7-Draw on information from multiple print or digital sources, demonstrating the ability to locate an answer to a question quickly or to solve a problem efficiently.

CCSS.ELA-LITERACY.SL.K-5.1-Engage effectively on a range of collaborative discussions (one-on-one, in groups, and teacher-led) with diverse partners on grades kindergarten through 5 topics and texts, building on other's ideas and expressing their own clearly.

CCSS.ELA-LITERACY.SL.K-5.5-Include multimedia components (e.g., graphics, sound) and visual displays in presentations when appropriate to enhance the development of main ideas or themes.

CCSS.ELA-LITERACY.SL.K-5.6-Adapt speech to a variety of contexts and tasks, using formal English when appropriate to task and situation.

C3Framework.D1.2.K-5.Identify disciplinary concepts and ideas associated with a compelling question that are open to different interpretations.

C3Framework.D2.Civ.8.K-5.Identify core civic virtues and democratic principles that guide government, society, and communities.

C3Framework.D3.1.K-5.Gather relevant information from multiple sources while using the origin, structure, and the context to guide the selection.

C3Framework.D3.4.3-5.Use evidence to develop claims in response to compelling questions.

C3Framework.D4.2.K-5.Construct explanations using reasoning, correct sequence, examples, and details with relevant information and data.

Activity: Students are divided into five collaborative groups and each group is assigned one of the following democratic principles: liberty, freedom, justice, equality, or common good. Through research and the evaluation of multiple primary sources, collaborative groups will determine the meaning of their assigned democratic principle and answer the compelling question "What does it mean to be an American?" from the perspective of their assigned democratic principle. The primary sources students may utilize should be age appropriate and may include: photographs, images, diaries, letters, pamphlets, notes, maps, charts, graphs, political cartoons, periodical articles (e.g., newspaper, journal, magazine), speeches, oral history, music, books/literature, blogs, or emails.

Collaborative Group Product and Assessment: After completing their research, collaborative groups will present their answer to the compelling question from the lens of their assigned democratic principle. Students will support their presentation with the research and evaluation of multiple primary sources. Collaborative group presentations will include a visual support (e.g., slide show, Prezi presentation, 3-D model, poster, or other visual aid). The number of supporting details and sources required should be grade-level appropriate. Classmates should be encouraged to ask questions to clarify their understanding of the democratic principles and the meaning of American citizenship. Students can be assessed on the academic content of their collaborative group presentation as well as the *Collaborative Group Rubric: Grades K-5.*

Sample Activity 2: Comparing the Past and Present: Grades 1-5

Compelling Question: How are we shaped by the past?

CCSS.ELA-LITERACY.RI.1-5.2-Determine two or more main ideas of a text and explain how they are supported by key details; summarize the text.

CCSS.ELA-LITERACY.RI.1-5.7-Draw on information from multiple print or digital sources, demonstrating the ability to locate an answer to a question quickly or to solve a problem efficiently.

CCSS.ELA-LITERACY.SL.1-5.5-Include multimedia components (e.g., graphics, sound) and visual displays in presentations when appropriate to enhance the development of main ideas or themes.

CCSS.ELA-LITERACY.SL.1-5.6-Adapt speech to a variety of contexts and tasks, using formal English when appropriate to task and situation.

CCSS.ELA-LITERACY.W.1-5.2-Write informative/explanatory texts to examine a topic and convey ideas and information clearly.

CCSS.ELA-LITERACY.W.1-5.7-Conduct short research projects that use several sources to build knowledge through investigation of different aspects of a topic.

C3Framework.D1.2.K-5.Identify disciplinary concepts and ideas associated with a compelling question that are open to different interpretations.

C3Framework.D2.Hist.2.K-5.Compare life in specific historical time periods to life today.

C3Framework.D2.Hist.10.K-5.Compare information provided by different historical sources about the past.

C3Framework.D3.1.K-5.Gather relevant information from multiple sources while using the origin, structure, and the context to guide the selection.

C3Framework.D3.2.3-5.Use distinction among fact and opinion to determine the credibility of multiple sources.

C3Framework.D3.3.3-5.Identify evidence that draws information from multiple sources in response to compelling questions.

<u>C3Framework.D4.2.K-5.</u>Construct explanations using reasoning, correct sequence, examples, and details with relevant information and data.

Activity: In order to have a better understanding of the past and its influence today, students will research and evaluate a historical topic of the past and compare/contrast it to its corresponding topic today using various primary sources (e.g., photographs, images, diaries, letters, pamphlets, notes, maps, charts, graphs, political cartoons, newspaper/ journal/magazine articles, speeches, oral history, music, books/literature, blogs, emails) and secondary sources. Historical and present day categories may include: work, war, education, roles of men and women, clothing, food, music and art, and homes and buildings.

A class field trip to a museum or local historical destination can be planned to allow students to conduct hands-on research. After conducting research, collaborative groups will determine "How are we shaped by the past?" from the perspective of their assigned topic.

Collaborative Group Product: Collaborative groups will create a mini-book with four parts: 1. Description and evaluation of the historical topic of the past; 2. Description and evaluation of the present day topic; 3. Venn diagram comparing and contrasting the topic of the past and present; and 4. Evaluation of how we are shaped by the past from the perspective of their assigned topic. Collaborative group mini-books should include visual pictures, images, or drawings to support findings and conclusions. More visual representations than words, sentences, or paragraphs should be expected for younger students. The number of supporting details and sources required should be adjusted to make the activity grade-level appropriate. Collaborative groups will present a summary of their finding to the class. Classmates should be encouraged to ask questions to clarify their understanding of how the past influences us today. Students can be assessed on the academic content of their collaborative group mini-book as well as the *Collaborative Group Rubric: Grades K-5.*

Sample Activity 3: Diversity in America: Grades 1-5

<u>Compelling Question:</u> How can our differences make America stronger?

<u>CCSS.ELA-LITERACY.RI.1-5.2</u>-Determine two or more main ideas of a text and explain how they are supported by key details; summarize the text.

<u>CCSS.ELA-LITERACY.RI.1-5.7</u>-Draw on information from multiple print or digital sources, demonstrating the ability to locate an answer to a question quickly or to solve a problem efficiently.

<u>CCSS.ELA-LITERACY.SL.1-5.1</u>-Engage effectively on a range of collaborative discussions (one-on-one, in groups, and teacher-led) with diverse partners on grades one through 5 topics and texts, building on other's ideas and expressing their own clearly.

<u>CCSS.ELA-LITERACY.SL.1-5.5</u>-Include multimedia components (e.g., graphics, sound) and visual displays in presentations when appropriate to enhance the development of main ideas or themes.

CCSS.ELA-LITERACY.SL.1-5.6-Adapt speech to a variety of contexts and tasks, using formal English when appropriate to task and situation.

CCSS.ELA-LITERACY.W.1-5.6-With some guidance and support from adults, use technology, including the Internet, to produce and publish writing as well as interact and collaborate with others.

CCSS.ELA-LITERACY.W.1-5.7-Conduct short research projects that use several sources to build knowledge through investigation of different aspects of a topic.

C3Framework.D1.2.K-5.Identify disciplinary concepts and ideas associated with a compelling question that are open to different interpretations.

C3Framework.D2.Geo.4.3-5.Explains how culture influences the way people modify and adapt to their environment.

C3Framework.D3.1.K-5.Gather relevant information from multiple sources while using the origin, structure, and the context to guide the selection.

C3Framework.D3.3.3-5.Identify evidence that draws information from multiple sources in response to compelling questions.

C3Framework.D4.2.K-5.Construct explanations using reasoning, correct sequence, examples, and details with relevant information and data.

Activity: Students will explore diversity in America. Younger students might explore diversity in their family, school, and community, while older students might explore diversity in their state and country. Collaborative groups will be assigned one of the following diversity categories: customs/traditions, music, art, literature, dance, or food. Collaborative groups will research and evaluate their assigned diversity category using various primary sources (e.g., photographs, images, diaries, letters, pamphlets, notes, maps, charts, graphs, political cartoons, newspaper/ journal/ magazine articles, speeches, oral history, music, books/literature, blogs, emails) and secondary sources. Based on the research and evaluation of their assigned diversity category, each collaborative group will determine an answer to the compelling question "How can our differences make America stronger?"

Collaborative Group Product: Collaborative groups will create and present a slide show (using PowerPoint, Google Docs, Prezi, or other slide show software program) to the class that answers the compelling question from the lens of their assigned diversity category. Collaborative group members must support their compelling question response with research and the evaluation of multiple sources. Classmates should be encouraged to ask questions to clarify their understanding of American diversity. Students can be assessed on the academic content of their collaborative group slide show as well as the *Collaborative Group Rubric: Grades K-5.*

Sample Activity 4: American Colonial Museum: Grades 3-5

Compelling Question: How does geography affect the way people live?

CCSS.ELA-LITERACY.RI.3-5.3-Explain the relationship or interactions between two or more individuals, events, ideas, or concepts in a historical, scientific, or technical text based on specific information in the text.

CCSS.ELA-LITERACY.RI.3-5.7-Draw on information from multiple print or digital sources, demonstrating the ability to locate an answer to a question quickly or to solve a problem efficiently.

CCSS.ELA-LITERACY.SL.3-5.1-Engage effectively on a range of collaborative discussions (one-on-one, in groups, and teacher-led) with diverse partners on grades 3 through 5 topics and texts, building on other's ideas and expressing their own clearly.

CCSS.ELA-LITERACY.SL.3-5.2-Summarize a written text read aloud or information presented in diverse media and formats, including visually, quantitatively, and orally.

CCSS.ELA-LITERACY.SL.3-5.5-Include multimedia components (e.g., graphics, sound) and visual displays in presentations when appropriate to enhance the development of main ideas or themes.

CCSS.ELA-LITERACY.SL.3-5.6-Adapt speech to a variety of contexts and tasks, using formal English when appropriate to task and situation.

CCSS.ELA-LITERACY.W.3-5.2-Write informative/explanatory texts to examine a topic and convey ideas and information clearly.

C3Framework.D1.2.3-5.Identify disciplinary concepts and ideas associated with a compelling question that are open to different interpretations.

C3Framework.D2.Eco.3.3-5.Identify examples of the variety of resources (human capital, physical capital, and natural resources) that are used to produce goods and services.

C3Framework.D2.Geo.4.3-5.Explains how culture influences the way people modify and adapt to their environment.

C3Framework.D2.Geo.6.3-5.Describe how environmental and cultural characteristics influence population distribution in specific places or regions.

C3Framework.D2.Geo.8.3-5.Explain how human settlements and movements relate to the locations and use of various natural resources.

C3Framework.D2.Hist.14.3-5.Explain the probable cause and effects of events and developments.

C3Framework.D3.1.3-5.Gather relevant information from multiple sources while using the origin, structure, and the context to guide the selection.

C3Framework.D3.2.3-5.Use distinctions among fact and opinion to determine the credibility of multiple sources.

C3Framework.D3.3.3-5.Identify evidence that draws information from multiple sources in response to compelling questions.

C3Framework.D3.4.3-5.Use evidence to develop claims in response to compelling questions.

C3Framework.D4.2.3-5.Construct explanations using reasoning, correct sequence, examples, and details with relevant information and data.

C3Framework.D4.2.3-5.Present a summary of arguments and explanations to others outside the classroom using print and oral technologies (e.g., posters, essays, letters, debates, speeches, reports) and digital technologies (e.g., Internet, social media, and digital documentary).

Activity: Collaborative groups will be assigned one of the following American colonies:

1. Massachusetts Bay/Plymouth Colony; 2. Connecticut Colony; 3. Rhode Island/Providence Plantations Colony; 4. New Hampshire Colony; 5. New York/New Amsterdam Colony; 6. New Jersey Colony; 7. Pennsylvania Colony; 8. Delaware Colony; 9. Virginia/Jamestown Colony; 10. Maryland Colony; 11. North Carolina Colony; 12. South Carolina Colony; or 13. Georgia Colony

Students will research and evaluate their assigned American colony using various primary sources (e.g., photographs, images, diaries, letters, pamphlets, notes, maps, charts, graphs, political cartoons, newspaper/ journal/magazine articles, speeches, oral history, music, books/literature, blogs, emails) and secondary sources. The compelling question "How does geography affect the way people live?" should be the focus of collaborative group research. Collaborative groups will determine how geography impacted the settlement of the thirteen original colonies and create a classroom museum exhibit for their assigned colony.

Collaborative Group Product: Collaborative groups create and present an exhibit for their assigned colony in a classroom American Colonial Museum. Students of a younger grade will be the audience of the museum exhibits. Requirements of the colonial exhibit will include: 1. A map showing the location and important geographical features of the colony; 2. A visual aid reflecting typical clothing of the colony; 3. A list of five words that best describe the colony; 4. A graph showing the population and ethnic/racial constitution of the colony; 5. A sample menu of a typical meal eaten in the colony; 6. A brief paragraph description of the colony's government; 7. A list of the typical jobs of colonial inhabitants; and 8. An additional three-dimensional visual aid that represents the colony (collaborative group's choice). All aspects of the collaborative group's colonial exhibit should be connected to the compelling question "How does geography affect the way people live?" Collaborative group members will act as docents for their colonial museum exhibit. Students can be assessed on the content of their museum exhibit displays and presentations as well as the *Collaborative Group Rubric: Grades K-5.*

Sample Activity 5: Making a Difference in Our Community Inquiry-Based Research: Grades K-2

Compelling Question: How can we make a difference in our community?

CCSS.ELA-LITERACY.RI.K-2.1-Ask and answer such questions as who, what, where, when, why, and how to demonstrate understanding of key details in a text.

CCSS.ELA-LITERACY.RI.K-2.7-Explain how specific images (e.g., a diagram showing how a machine works) contribute to and clarify a text.

CCSS.ELA-LITERACY.SL.K-2.1-Engage effectively on a range of collaborative discussions (one-on-one, in groups, and teacher-led) with diverse partners on kindergarten through grade 2 topics and texts, building on other's ideas and expressing their own clearly.

CCSS.ELA-LITERACY.SL.K-2.6-Produce complete sentences when appropriate to task and situation in order to provide requested detail or clarification.

CCSS.ELA-LITERACY.W.K-2.7-Participate in shared research and writing (e.g., read a number of books on a single topic to produce a report; record science observations).

C3Framework.D1.2.K-2.Identify disciplinary concepts and ideas associated with a compelling question.

C3Framework.D2.Civ.6.K-2.Describe how communities work to accomplish common tasks, establish responsibilities, and fulfill roles of authority.

C3Framework.D2.Civ.11.K-2.Explain how people can work together to make decisions in the classroom.

C3Framework.D3.1.K-2.Gather relevant information from one or two sources while using the origin and structure to guide the selection.

C3Framework.D4.2.K-2.Construct explanations using correct sequence and relevant information.

C3Framework.D4.5.K-2.Ask and answer questions about explanations.

Activity: Students will participate in a student inquiry-based research project. The compelling question focus for this collaborative group activity is "How can we make a difference in our community?" However, *any* compelling question or topic focus can be used in a similar inquiry-based research activity. Simply follow the steps outlined below.

Step 1: What do we know? [1] As a class, students generate a list of what they know about their community. All student responses are written or typed by the teacher and displayed in the class.

Step 2: How do we know? [2] Students identify *how* they know about their community. Similarly, all student responses are written or typed by the teacher and displayed in the class. This step will create a working list of the types of sources student can use to conduct research.

Step 3: What else do students want to know?/What do we want to learn? Students will ask questions about their community. What else do they want to know that they don't already know? All student questions will be written down and displayed in the class. This is a critical step and the foundation for the research activity. Student questions will drive class research. The teacher will group questions of similar content together into larger categories. The students who authored questions in the same category will form a collaborative group.

Step 4: How do we get answers to our questions? [3] Working in collaborative groups, students discuss and determine how to get answers to their questions. While books can be one source, students should be encouraged to think beyond book sources. Collaborative groups will look back at the class generated working list of sources created in Step 2. What types of sources can collaborative groups add to the list? Internet websites? Pictures? Interviews? Visiting community sites? Newspaper articles? Town historical society? Town hall documents? Maps? Other images? The collaborative group will share their suggested sources with the class and the teacher will add their ideas to the original source list created in Step 2.

Step 5: Collaborative groups conduct research. Using their student generated questions and suggested source list as guides, students will conduct research as a collaborative group. If beneficial, the teacher can schedule guest speakers for the class to interview (e.g., key town community members). Students may conduct interviews with family members and school staff in order to obtain answers to their questions. The class may take community field trips to conduct research as well.

Step 6: Collaborative groups determine and complete any research that is missing. Collaborative groups will review the student-generated questions to determine if any of their questions were unanswered.[4] With teacher guidance, the collaborative groups will determine what addition research they need to conduct. Collaborative groups will complete any research necessary to answer their questions.

Step 7: Students complete a collaborative group product to showcase their research findings. Students can showcase their research findings in a multitude of ways, including: creating a PowerPoint or digital slide presentation, authoring pages to add to a class book, designing patches to be added to a class quilt, etc. Regardless of the product, collaborative groups will present their research findings to the class. Classmates should be encouraged to ask questions to clarify their understanding of each collaborative group's research findings. Students can be assessed on the academic content of their collaborative group product as well as the Collaborative Group Rubric: Grades K-5.

Step 8: Taking informed action as a class. Based on the research findings of collaborative groups, students will brainstorm ways they can make a difference in their community (e.g., write a letter to the town/city newspaper editor, participate in a community clean-up project, donate food to a local food bank, organize a clothing drive). The teacher will write or type student suggestions. After all student-generated ideas are proposed, discussed, and vetted, students will select the way they would like to make a difference in their community by taking a class vote. Students will participate in the class community project winning idea.

CONCLUSION

Final Thought

*"I fear the day that technology will surpass our human interaction.
The world will have a generation of idiots." –Albert Einstein?* [1]

The quote above, attributed to Albert Einstein, was repeatedly posted on Facebook in 2014. Usually the quote was accompanied by two pictures: one of Einstein and another of young people staring at their technological devices. Along with many others, I assert technological overuse is impeding our children's soft skill development. The quote predicts this concept too perfectly. While I wanted to believe Einstein said it, each time I saw the quote, I felt suspicious. In an attempt to verify the quote's authenticity, I searched it on quoteinvestigator.com, a website numerous media outlets have used to verify quotes. Quoteinvestigator.com concluded "there is no substantive evidence" that Einstein made the statement. [2] According to Garson O'Toole of quoteinvestigator.com, the quote does not appear in Princeton University's comprehensive collection of Einstein quotes and the quote, seeming too modern, was in circulation in 2012. [3]

I do not want to see our children's soft skills impaired by technological overuse. Teaching soft skills in the classroom and supporting students as they practice soft skill development through collaborative group activities and assessments is one way to counteract technological overuse. It isn't the only solution though. Increased collaborative group activities must be paired with clear technological use boundaries set and modeled by parents and educators. We need to be clear with our children. Technology is amazing and wonderful, but technological overuse is detrimental. Moderation is the key.

As educators, we are given the opportunity to challenge our students to create, think, and learn. What we do in the classroom impacts the future. Let's take the time to support our students' essential soft skill development. This is what our students need. This is what society needs. This is what the future needs. I'm ready for the challenge. Will you join me?

For those that circulated the above referenced technology quote attributed to Einstein, I am wondering if a chocolate frosted cupcake with a lime green "T" might help.

NOTES

Introduction

1. "Re: Stake Your Claim." Web log comment. *Cupcake Canasta*. Blogspot, 10 Mar. 2011. Web. 27 June 2014.

2. & 3. Hofmann, Janell B. "To My 13-Year-Old, An IPhone Contract From Your Mom, With Love." *Huff Post*. Huffingtonpost.com, 28 Dec. 2012. Web. 25 June 2014.

Chapter 1

1., 2., 6. & 12. Stout, Hillary. "Antisocial Networking?" *New York Times*. Newyorktimes.com, 30 Apr. 2010. Web. 28 June 2014.

3., 11., 17. & 22. Ludden, Jennifer. "Teen Texting Soars; Will Social Skills Suffer?" *NPR*. Npr.org, 20 Apr. 2010. Web. 25June 2014.

4., 14., 23., 24., 29., 30., 31., 32., 33., 34. & 35. Dokoupil, Tony. "Is the Internet Making Us Crazy? What the New Research Saya." *Newsweek*. Newsweek.com, 9 July 2012. Web. 26 June 2014.

5., 18., 19., 20., 25., 26. & 27. *Teens and Technology*. Rep. Pewresearchcenter.org, 13 Mar. 2013. Web. 30 June 2014.

7., 8., 28., 36. & 38. Brown, Cecilia. "Are We Becoming More Socially Awkward? An Analysis of the Relationship Between Technological Communication Use and Social Skills in College Students. (2013). *Psychology Honors Papers*. Paper 40.

9., 10., 13., 16., 37., 39. & 40. Bindley, Katherine. "When Children Text All Day, What Happens to Their Social Skills." *Huffington Post*. Huffingtonpost.com, 10 Dec. 2010. Web. 25 June 2014.

15. Fox 9. "Help a teacher out and share this pic." *Facebook.com* 29 November 2013. Web 29 July 2014.

21. "Ring the Bells: More Smartphones in Students' Hands Ahead of Back-to-School Season." *Nielson*. Nielson.com, 29 Oct. 2013. Web. 27 June 2014.

41. Hofmann, Janell B. "To My 13-Year-Old, An IPhone Contract From Your Mom, With Love." *Huff Post*. Huffingtonpost.com, 28 Dec. 2012. Web. 25 June 2014.

Chapter 2

1., 14., 15.,19., 20. & 21. White, Martha C. "The Real Reason New College Grads Can't Get Hired." *Time*. Time.com, 10 Nov. 2013. Web. 25 June 2014.

2., 8., 12., 16. & 17. Vasel, Kathryn B. "The Skills Employers Wish College Grads Had." *FOX Business*. Foxbusiness.com, 30 Jan. 2014. Web. 29 June 2014.

3. & 11. Giang, Vivian. "Why Gen Y Workers Have No Idea What Their Managers Expect From Them." *Business Insider*. Businessinsider.com, 3 Sept. 2013. Web. 25 June 2014.

4., 5. & 6. Salpeter, Miriam. "5 Soft Skills to Showcase in an Interview." *US News and World Report*. USnewsandworldreport.com, 20 Mar. 2013. Web. 28 June 2014.

7., 9., 10. & 18. "Why Employers Say Millennials Can't Get a Job." *KCRA*. Krca.com, 11 Feb. 2014. Web. 29 June 2014.

13. Fontaine, Tom. "RMU Poll: Many Worry Young Adults Lack Social Skill Due to Technology." *Trib LIVE*. Trib Total Media, 27 Mar. 2014. Web. 29 June 2014.

22. McCafferty, Dennis. "Managers Say Employees Lack Critical Skills." *Baseline Driving Business Success With Technology*. Baselinemag.com, 28 Mar. 2013. Web. 29 June 2014.

Chapter 3

1. Doyle, Alison. "Top 10 Communication Skills." *About.com Job Searching*. Jobsearch.about.com. Web. 26 June 2014.

2. Morley, Miranda. "Examples of Business Communication Skills." *Demand Media Houston Chronicle*. Hearst Newspapers, LLC. Web. 30 June 2014.

3., 4., 7., 8. & 10. MindTools.com. (2014) Conflict Resolution: Resolving Conflict Rationally and Effectively. [Online] Available from: http://www.mindtools.com/pages/article/morale.htm. [Accessed: June 25, 2014].

5. "Teamwork Skills: Being an Effective Group Member." *Centre for Teaching Excellence*. Uwaterloo. ca. Web. 27 June 2014.

6., 9. & 12. "Effective Communication-Improving Your Social Skills." *Anxiety BC*. Anxietybc.com. Web. 27 June 2014.

11., 17. & 18. "Tips for Effective Teamwork." *Melbourne Law School Legal Academic Skills Center*. Law. unimelb.edu.au. Web. 25 June 2014.

13. & 15. Berteig, Mishkin. "Seven Essential Teamwork Skills." *Agile Advice*. Agileadvice.com, 12 Oct. 2009. Web. 30 June 2014.

14. Kokemuller, Neil. "Good Skills for Teamwork." *Demand Media Houston Chronicle*. Hearst Newspapers, LLC. Web. 30 June 2014.

16. "Teamwork & Collaboration Skills." *University of Strathclyde Glasgow*. Strath.ac.uk. Web. 30 June 2014.

Chapter 4

1. Anderson, Margaret. "Mind Styles-Anthony Gregorc." *SUNY Courtland Faculty Web*. SUNY Courtland, n.d. Web. 22 July 2014.

2. *Four Types of Learning Styles*. Boise State University, n.d. Web. 22 July 2014.

Chapter 7

1., 2., 3 & 4. Rogovin, Paula. "First Graders Research Stuffed Animals and Learn about Their World." *Social Studies and the Young Learner*. National Council for the Social Studies. September/October 2011.

Final Thought

1. WPLR 99.1 New Haven. "Aaaaaaaannnd we're there (Chaz&AJ)" *Facebook.com* 12 June 2014. Web 25 June 2014.

2. & 3. O'Toole, Garson. "I Fear the Day That Technology Will Surpass Our Human Interaction." *Quote Investigator*. Quoteinvestigator.com, 19 Mar. 2013. Web. 27 June 2014.

www.ingramcontent.com/pod-product-compliance
Lightning Source LLC
Chambersburg PA
CBHW082111070326
40689CB00052B/4550